Contents

Foreword

In Pennal there's an Wtra'r Beddau (*'lane of the graves'*) and on Anglesey, a Bodgadfa (*'place of battle'*). Place names and legends associated with old battles pepper Wales. Professor Bedwyr Lewis Jones used to say that we are too fond of inventing stories to explain gruesome place names!

But no matter how many local stories there are about old battles, scant attention is paid to the true history of battles in Wales. Few sites are signposted; few have interpretation boards to keep the memory alive.

Battles *for* Wales is the topic explored in this volume. There have been other battles on this country's soil, but those discussed here are to do with protecting and securing our land and our rights as a people.

1. *Llywelyn Fawr in Conwy;*
2. *Llywelyn ap Gruffudd, Llanymddyfri*

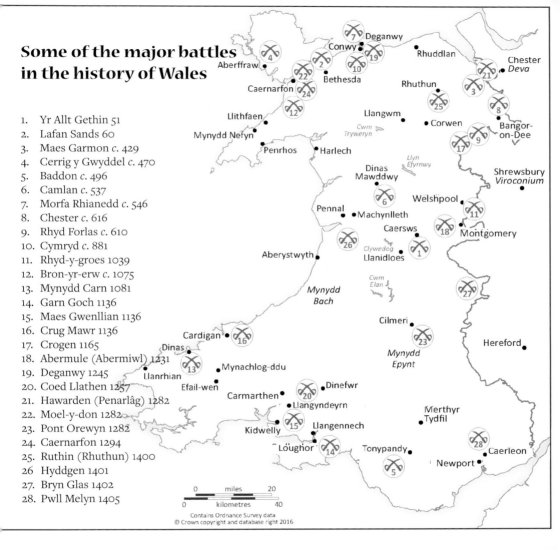

Some of the major battles in the history of Wales

1. Yr Allt Gethin 51
2. Lafan Sands 60
3. Maes Garmon *c.* 429
4. Cerrig y Gwyddel *c.* 470
5. Baddon *c.* 496
6. Camlan *c.* 537
7. Morfa Rhianedd *c.* 546
8. Chester *c.* 616
9. Rhyd Forlas *c.* 610
10. Cymryd *c.* 881
11. Rhyd-y-groes 1039
12. Bron-yr-erw *c.* 1075
13. Mynydd Carn 1081
14. Garn Goch 1136
15. Maes Gwenllian 1136
16. Crug Mawr 1136
17. Crogen 1165
18. Abermule (Abermiwl) 1231
19. Deganwy 1245
20. Coed Llathen 1257
21. Hawarden (Penarlâg) 1282
22. Moel-y-don 1282
23. Pont Orewyn 1282
24. Caernarfon 1294
25. Ruthin (Rhuthun) 1400
26. Hyddgen 1401
27. Bryn Glas 1402
28. Pwll Melyn 1405

Contains Ordnance Survey data
© Crown copyright and database right 2016

Yr Allt Gethin

Location: Caersws area
Battle: Brythons (Caradog)/Romans
Date: AD 51

Although the islands of the Celts in Britain were at the north-western edge of the Roman Empire, they were not remote to ships from the Mediterranean during the Bronze Age and Iron Age. Through the study of ancient shipwrecks on the shores of Llŷn, of burial practices, of DNA evidence, of archaeological remains, and of the spread of Celtic languages along the shores of the Atlantic Ocean from Portugal to the Scottish Islands, we know that there were strong commercial and cultural connections along the coast, and that a gradual and sustained colonisation has occurred since the retreat of the last Ice Age.

Long before the Romans and their revolutionary road construction technology changed the course of the world, the Celts came to Wales, Cornwall, Ireland and Scotland from the Mediterranean. Trade routes and culture were sustained for centuries and thereby tribes spread eastwards, following the main rivers of the Continent.

Caesar would have known about the trade in stone implements, and in bronze, tin, copper and iron artefacts that took place for hundreds of years between the islands of Britain and southern Europe. He also knew of the gold and salt reserves in Britain, and the abundant corn grown on the plains. While the Roman legions were fighting in Gaul, some of the Belgae tribe of Celts (from today's north-east France and Belgium) migrated over the channel to what is now Kent. In the midst of subduing Gaul, Caesar and his ships followed those same routes and landed north of Dover in 55 BC. He stayed there for a week before returning to the Continent with his confident statement, 'Vene, vidi, vici'. But he was far from defeating the Celts of these islands, of course, despite returning in the following year.

The Roman conquest occurred in AD 43 when Plautius sailed across the channel with four legions and auxiliary forces, a total of 40,000 troops. As John Davies explains in *A History of Wales* – although the islands of Britain were only a thirtieth of the territory of the Roman Empire, it

Part of the Roman legionary barracks, Caerleon

was necessary to deploy a tenth of their armies for centuries to defend themselves here.

By AD 47, the Brythons (the Celtic tribes of southern Britain) south of the Fosse Way – the Roman road from Lincoln to Exeter – were under the control of Rome. But this was not a trouble-free border. Beyond it were the Silures, a tribe in south-east Wales who were a constant thorn in the Empire's side. Caradog (*Caratacus* in Latin) was their leader; he had joined them after losing his kingdom south of the Fosse Way, following years of fighting.

The Romans soon realised that the flat land of the Severn and Dee valleys separates the hills of northern England from the hill country of Wales. They pushed ahead to control this area by defeating the Cornovii tribe in about AD 47 and establishing a military fort in Wroxeter (*Viroconium*) to house a legion of 5,500. Of the three permanent legionary fortresses in Britain, two were on the Welsh border: Chester in the north and Caerleon in the south.

Although the Romans had far greater resources and experience than the Brython armies, the countryside and style of fighting were new. Caradog was a guerrilla fighter. He attacked military regiments in forests and steep valleys and as they crossed rivers, and then retreated like mountain mist before the main legions arrived. His men did not form orderly ranks on the battlefield and fight to the end. It was hard to know where his main camp was and where he would strike next, and he was impossible to catch.

In AD 49 the Romans established a powerful military base at Gloucester. Caradog retreated to the territories of the Ordovices and Deceangli in north Wales, focusing his attacks on the legions stationed in the northern part of the Severn valley. He realised the importance of retaining land occupied by the Brythons; there was nowhere else left to retreat. The Roman general Ostorius had convened two legions of soldiers in Wroxeter. Caradog had some 30,000 warriors of his own. Gradually, he planned a way to draw the Romans away from their stronghold on the plains and face his men on the rugged mountains slopes of Wales. This was the great battle that would decide the future of Wales and all the land of the Brythons. If he won, Caradog could drive the Romans back into the sea.

Caradog knew that the Romans were keen to find out the exact location of his military base. Three hill forts are known as Caer Garadog in Wales and the borders. Two are on Shropshire hills (Grid Ref. 477 953, near Church Stretton; Grid Ref. 310 758, near Chapel Lawn). The one in north Wales is in the land of the Deceangli, near Llanfihangel Glyn Myfyr (Grid Ref. 968 479).

It's possible – even very likely – that these sites are linked to other battles and periods of Caradog's history, but none is suitable as the location of the last great battle. Fortunately, the historian Tacitus recorded a detailed description of this final battle. History is written by the victors is the saying but, as one Irishman said, it's the losers who compose the songs. Two of the forts are too close to Wroxeter, and the other too far away. Moreover, the detailed geographical picture we get from Tacitus matches none of the three locations above.

According to an analysis by Martin Hackett of the AD 51 battle, Caradog's army and Ostorius Scapula's did not engage haphazardly. Caradog had chosen his ground carefully: a place where he would, for a number of reasons, be most likely to defeat the Romans; he knew he

would not get another chance. The historian favours Cefn Carnedd and the hills near Caersws and Llandinam in the western Severn valley.

There, the valley bottom extends almost to Wroxeter in the east and affords a convenient way for the Romans to send out scouts, establish temporary camps and see the lie of the land during the two years before the battle. All the while Caradog's guerrillas plagued them continuously. It was vital for the Brythons to lure the legions out of their stronghold and to trap them into believing that they were facing the usual raid against a fort.

According Tacitus's description, the Brythons were on a fortified hilltop with stone walls to protect them. He describes Caradog as darting here and there, inspiring them to regain their freedom. The Romans faced a river at the foot of this hill, and Caradog's superior position would have struck fear into them. Yet the legionnaires showed their typical discipline by forming a 'military tortoise' (a *'testudo'*) with their shields to break through the walls as a hail of stones and javelins fell on them. Then it was hand-to-hand combat and gradually the Brythons retreated up the slope before, in the end, breaking ranks. Caradog's family were captured, but he managed to flee to what is now northern England where he was betrayed and delivered to the Romans by the queen of the Brigantes.

He was reunited with his family in captivity in Rome, and pleaded before Caesar to recognise him as a Brythonic king doing his duty: fighting for his land and people. The Romans were honourable enough to allow him some freedom in their city, but he never saw the Welsh hills again.

In the description by Tacitus, we see the cunning of Caradog as he manages to draw the legions 45 miles from the security of Wroxeter. Opposite his chosen battleground is a low, small hill fort – Cefn Carnedd – and this may have been the bait in the trap. Its slopes would not have been much of an obstacle to an organised, experienced Roman army. The Brythons would have given the impression to the Wroxeter scouts that they had located the main Brython fortress. Constant guerrilla attacks over two years would have drawn their attention higher and higher up the Severn valley and duped them into thinking this was Caradog's stronghold. The scouts would have returned to Wroxeter certain that the gradual slopes of Cefn Carnedd, its isolation, and relatively small size, would not pose much of an obstacle to them. They would still have prepared thoroughly and seen that there were sufficient troops to take part. It was an opportunity to quash the Brython uprising and catch Caradog.

As part of preparations, Scapula would have built a fort to defend the legion's encampment at Caersws. It was not too late for the Romans to turn back from there if their scouts suspected that they were being led into a trap. Caradog must have exercised strict discipline to prevent his troops from attacking too soon, and to keep them concealed in the hills and valleys towards Llandinam, while still giving the impression that preparations were being made for a fight at the small fort on the summit of Cefn Carnedd.

The river Carno runs towards the Severn below Cefn Carnedd; above their confluence there are fords and their beds are stony, full of flat stones. The Brythons used these stones to create defences on the lower slopes, and also to build rough walls on the upper slopes and ridges higher up the valley.

The most likely location that corresponds to the description in Tacitus, and which allows for routes used by Brython horses and vehicles to make a getaway, is Allt Gethin, just behind and above Llandinam. The slopes descend

1. Severn valley under Allt Gethin; 2. Part of the fort, Caersws; 3. Severn bridge, Caersws

steeply down the valley – too steep for Roman horsemen. Martin Hackett's achievement is that he has found the perfect location for 'the Battle of Caer Garadog' – with the irony that there is no fortress there – and that another fort was used to deceive and lure the Romans.

When Scapula realised the extent of the deception, Tacitus records the fear it caused. But it was too late to turn back. His soldiers, plagued by losses from relentless guerrilla attacks, had seen the enemy and their blood was up. It is likely that Scapula would have had between 20,000 and 25,000 troops under his command. There may well have been more warriors on Caradog's side.

We can infer this sequence of events at the battle of Allt Gethin: Scapula and his legions leave the camp at Caersws, heading for Cefn Carnedd fort; Caradog calls his chosen forces from that fortress and drives the ranks down the slopes to the lowest defences to face the river; then, reserve forces emerge along the hills' ridges, striking fear into the heart of the Romans; the Romans cross the fords with no trouble but, once they arrive within the range of the Brython slings and spears, gaps would start appearing in the ranks;

the Romans create a *testudo* – this means locking their shields to form an iron roof over their heads. They would test the strength of the *testudo* by placing a soldier on horseback on top. It was this tactic that eventually carried the day. Slowly and laboriously, and with large losses, hundreds of the Romans managed to ascend the slopes, driving the Brythons back onto the ridges. When Caradog saw that the battle had been lost, he was able to escape from there along the hills of what is now Montgomeryshire to plan his next fight.

Menai Strait

Location: 1. Lafan Sands; 2. Y Felinheli
Battle: Brythons of Anglesey/Romans
Date: 1. AD 60; 2. AD 78

Caradog's defeat was not the final nail in the coffin of Brythonic freedom and readiness to oppose the Romans. In AD 52, the Silures defeated a whole legion in south-east Wales, and the tribes there were not forced into submission until about AD 75, with a permanent civic and military presence in Caerwent and Caerleon (*Isca*). As John Davies says, 'The task of subduing Wales proved long and costly. There were at least thirteen campaigns in Wales and its borders between AD 48 and 79'.

Part of a druidic circle above Penmaenmawr

One of the most well known, and perhaps the most remarkable, was a raid in AD 60 – authorised by the Emperor Nero himself – to attack Anglesey. It wasn't the Brythonic armies that concerned the Romans there, but the druids, the tribes' intellectual and spiritual leaders.

The Romans had come across the druidic religion while conquering Gaul and had noted the hold it had over the Celts. As well as holding ceremonies to please the gods, they were the depositary of the tribes' history. Their methods were oral, and written Welsh literature and historical chronicles were rare until the ninth century. As the tribe depended on memory, that memory had to be detailed and remarkable, and within the ranks of the druids there were two groups: bards and priests. The bards' work was to spend many years learning and committing to memory the tribe's memory hoard. Social history, legends, the ancestry of kings, and the feats of heroes and warriors were all stored in their memories. Hearing their

history from the druid-bards and being assured that the gods were on their side by the druid-priests inspired the Celts to fight and survive. No enemy was too great for them once they had been so inflamed. The Romans knew from experience that by killing their druids the memory and spirit of the Celts would be shattered.

By this period, it appears that the Brython druids' centres were in oak groves on Anglesey. This western island was protected by mountains and the armies of the Ordovices. Once again, the Romans were shrewd enough to realise there was a direct route to Anglesey through a weak spot in the defences of north Wales: along the coast from Chester to the Menai Strait. By AD 78, the legion had built a road from Chester to Segontium (Caernarfon) with two 'overnight' forts on the route, Varis, near Bodfari, and Kanovium (Caerhun), guarding the ford across the river Conwy. Once again, the Romans blazed a trail that was followed by many armies in their quests to defeat and capture the Welsh and their country.

From AD 59 to 61, the general Suetonius Paulinus penetrated further and further north-west to attack Anglesey. After crossing the river Conwy, he climbed to Bwlch y Ddeufaen. From there he could see the Menai Strait, Anglesey, and the Lafan Sands: the treacherous crossing at low tide. According to tradition, this beach was largely dry land until the sixth century, when large parts of the west coast of Britain – from Cumbria to South Wales – subsided.

The Lafan Sands was used continuously as a crossing place to Anglesey from the end of the Age of the Princes up to the end of the drovers' period and the building of Telford's Menai Bridge in 1826. The narrowest crossing point was in the Beaumaris area, and once again we can presume that the Romans led the way where subsequent strangers followed.

Tacitus chronicles Paulinus' raid and he gives a dramatic description of the attack on Anglesey:

> On the opposite shore stood the opposing army, bristling with armed warriors. Women dressed in funereal

1. Across the Lafan Sands to Anglesey;
2. Bwlch y Ddeufaen; 3. Segontium

black darted to and fro between the ranks, waving firebrands, their hair streaming in the wind, dishevelled. All around them were rows of Druids, their arms raised to the heavens, intoning a stream of imprecations which terrified the soldiers to their very cores. The novelty of this form of fighting rooted them to the spot, frozen, their muscles paralysed, sitting targets for enemy fire. Suetonius was facing a crisis of spirit. He urged his warriors, who had conquered the whole world, not to 'be afraid of a bunch of women and fanatics'. The legion's standards drove forward into battle and they mowed down all who stood in their way, tossing the enemies into their own fires. Those conquered were quelled forcefully, their groves, which had been consecrated to inhuman superstition, destroyed.

From the records, we see that the Romans had prepared a fleet of shallow, flat-bottomed vessels for crossing the Strait. The mounted soldiers followed by fording the current as best they could, or by swimming with their horses. Once again, the ranks of the Brythons were devastated when faced with experienced and disciplined Roman troops, and the slaughter on the island was terrible. Sacred sites and temples were destroyed, altars wrecked and many of the druids killed.

Allegedly, some managed to survive and escape. Some fled to Ireland and the Isle of Man. Not all the learning and memory was lost. The old religion continued to be practiced, but covertly. Later, some Latin writers view the druids' wondrous knowledge – their ability as mathematicians, astronomers and storytellers – with respect.

In the midst of the despoilment of Anglesey in AD 60, the legion received news that Buddug and her daughters and the Iceni tribe had risen in rebellion in south-eastern Britain. The Romans had refused to recognise Buddug as queen of the Iceni after she lost her husband, which would have been the natural order of things to the Celts. She was flogged and her daughters raped. This sparked the uprising and the women who led it. The Roman roads were used against the conquerors themselves, and Colchester and London were burned. Suetonius

The Menai Strait east of the Menai Bridge

hurried back from Anglesey to defeat the insurgents with his legion.

Then in AD 78 the Romans returned to Anglesey, led by Agricola. This time they were sallying forth from more secure forts, and it's possible that their Straits crossing may have been made closer to Segontium – at Llanidan, perhaps, or in the Menai Bridge (*Porthaethwy*) area. Gradually, Roman roads spread across Wales, linking a network of forts together, and a few centuries of peace ensued. The remains at Caerleon, at Caerwent and along the border to Wroxeter and Chester stand as a tribute to the valour of the people of Wales, who managed to retain their lands in the face of the might of the one of the world's greatest empires.

Maes Garmon

Location: Maes Garmon near Mold
Battle: Welsh/Saxon
Date: about 429

It is a Welsh tradition, noted by Bede and also appearing in Constantius's Life of Garmon, that 'Saint Garmon' led the Christian Welsh to victory against the pagan Saxons and Picts in 429. According to Bede, the Welsh troops were baptised by this churchman before concealing themselves behind trees in a narrow valley. As the enemies reached a clearing, intending to ambush them, the Welsh leaped into view and, following the guidance of the saint, shouted 'Hallelujah!' three times while brandishing their weapons and flags. Their voices echoed from the rocks, leading their attackers to believe that there were numerous legions ready to fight them. In their panic, they dropped their weapons and spoils on the ground and rushed back the way they had come, but some fell into a nearby river and drowned. The Welsh won the day without having to fire a shot or shed a drop of blood.

Bede was a monk and, of course, he had a moral problem in reporting a Christian saint leading an army to war. This was not a problem for some Welsh hagiographers – the story about Saint David urging Welsh soldiers to each wear a leek from a field adjacent to a battlefield so they knew each other when facing an English army is very familiar. As Charles-Edwards observes, there are elements of the biblical walls of Jericho collapsing to the sound of trumpets in Bede's telling. Bede showing that a bishop led an army would make the story respectable in the eyes of the church.

Bede does not locate the 'battle' geographically, but the suggestion by Archbishop Ussher in the seventeenth century is that it has happened on farmland at Maes Garmon, near Mold (*Yr Wyddgrug*). In 1736, a member of the gentry named Nehemiah Griffith, of Rhual estate, erected a column on the land in order to remember the fight in the clearing. Engraved in Latin on the column are the words 'In the year CCCCXX the Picts and Saxons made war with their combined army against the Britons in this country known as Maes Garmon today.

The memorial at Maes Garmon

When the host descended to battle the apostolic generals of the Britons, namely Garmon, Lupus and Christ were present in the camp, and thrice exclaimed Aleluia. The enemy's army was struck with awe: the Britons triumphed: destroyed their enemies without bloodshed: the victory gained by faith, not by force of arms.'

Martin Hackett has difficulty trying to square Bede's story with the terrain of the Alun valley near Mold. Where are the rocky slopes and narrow valley, and a river with enough depth to drown fleeing soldiers? Other scholars relocate the story to the Dee valley near Valle Crucis, asserting that the Pillar of Eliseg originally commemorated this battle. But an archaeological survey has turned up human bones in mass graves at Maes Garmon. Evidence points to a battle having taken place near Mold and it's possible that two stories have been conflated at this site because of the place name.

Who was the 'Saint Garmon' associated with these stories? According to some writers, this character was Saint Germanus, bishop of Auxerre in France. He came to Britain with his companion, Bishop Lupus (*Bleiddian* in Welsh) of Troyes, in 429 to protect the unity of the Church of Rome by meeting ecclesiastics in St. Albans. While they were here, the Brythons were attacked by an alliance of Picts and Saxons and, according to legend, the two bishops played their part in protecting the Christians and their lands.

Another difficulty emerges, according to the expert on place names Melville Richards. Germanus does not normally cymricise to give 'Garmon'. Here is an example, he says, of the 'insatiable desire' of some scholars to link the names of Welsh saints with Latin names. He agrees that the Garmon of the Welsh tradition is different from Germanus Auxerre. The Saint Garmon of legend ministered in many parishes called Llanarmon in north and central Wales, and is associated with Benlli Gawr and Vortigern (in Welsh, *Gwrtheyrn*). Richards agrees with Ifor Williams that Garmon is an indigenous Welsh word, stemming from – very interestingly – *garm*, 'a shout'. In *Hanes Gruffudd ap Cynan* (The History of Gruffudd ap Cynan) the 'Hallelujah' battle is located in the Nant y Garth pass near Llanarmon-yn-Iâl (near the Tomen y Rhodwydd site). The geography there – a narrow valley, echoing rock and a deep river – is a further indication that two stories have been interwoven.

From what we know, we can be reasonably sure that the Welsh had some success in battle against the Saxons (and the Picts) who were attacking their provinces in the fifth century. There are strong indications that some Welsh saints blessed armies and ignited their spirits. There was a battle at Maes Garmon, near Mold, and bodies of soldiers are buried nearby, but we cannot be certain of its date. As it is close to routes used for attack by Northumbrian or Mercian Saxons, it may well be that there was a battle between the Welsh and an army from England. If there was a struggle in the early fifth century in an area as far west as the Alun valley, we can also be pretty confident that the Welsh carried the day on that occasion.

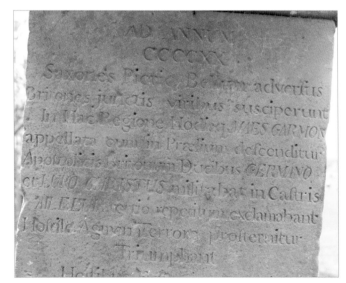

Cerrig y Gwyddel

Location: near Rhyd y Foty (Map Ref. 4072)
Battle: Welsh/Irish
Date: about 470

In the prehistoric period there was continuous navigation across the Irish Sea, described as the 'Celtic Mediterranean' by one historian. That activity did not come to an end when the power of Rome reached the west coast of Wales; rather, the Roman military was deployed to prevent uncontrolled Irish raids and their colonisation of western peninsulas.

But in 383 Macsen Wledig (*Magnus Maximus*) left Wales, taking the regiments that had been stationed in Welsh forts with him across Europe to fight for control of the Western Empire. He was successful there for the first few years, but he left Wales defenceless in his wake. The Irish had already settled in the south-west and north-west of Britain. In 405, Nial the Irishman pillaged the coast of Wales. This happened more often over the following century and, gradually, Roman Britain disappeared and the Welsh nation and language appeared.

A number of small kingdoms, each with its own king, emerged in Wales and gradually the smaller kingdoms were absorbed by the stronger kings. According to Nennius, Cunedda (about 440) and the Men of the Old North sailed from Strathclyde to north Wales and established a lineage of strong rulers: the kings and princes of Gwynedd, from Maelgwn Gwynedd to Llywelyn II. Jewellery from the river Forth area has been found in the Pant-y-saer *cromlech* (dolmen) in Anglesey, and rectangular graves of the Strathclyde type discovered in the Vale of Clwyd.

It is known that cavalry from Wales went to support the Gododdin tribe (the Brythons in the Edinburgh area) in their raid against the Anglo-Saxons at Catterick (*Catraeth*, in Welsh) in about 600. There is now enough evidence to show that Cunedda and his eight sons migrated to north Wales around 440, largely to fill the gap left by the Roman legions and so establish strong kingdoms as a bulwark against the Irish. Nevertheless, names like Llŷn and Dinllaen show that Irish influence on the shores of Gwynedd continued for some time. Also during these centuries, saints were constantly coming and going between Ireland, Wales, and the other Celtic countries. Western maritime trade routes were also re-established. The advent of Germanic tribes in the east of Britain did not break the link between Wales and the rest of Europe. Pottery from the Black Sea was discovered in the court of Maelgwn Gwynedd in Deganwy.

The Irish influence lasted longer in Pembroke and *Brycheiniog* (Breconshire). Brychan Brycheiniog king of that province in the fifth century, was of Irish royal descent. His centre was a crannog on Llangorse Lake; a crannog is a fortified

Cerrig y Gwyddel battlefield

island built on poles in a lake and they were common in Ireland.

Traces of crannogs have been found in Llyn Llydaw at the foot of Snowdon, and many Celtic roundhouses in north-west Wales are still called 'Cytiau'r Gwyddelod' ('Irish huts'). But the Irish did not get the chance to gain enough land for long enough to actually govern in Gwynedd. The archaeologist Rhys Mwyn shows that there is evidence that some of the 'Cytiau'r Gwyddelod' in Wales go back to the Bronze Age, and some are still being used in the Roman period. Often they were farms, as at Tŷ Mawr, Holyhead (*Caergybi*) and Meillionnydd and Rhiw in Llŷn. The name may give a false impression of extensive migration from Ireland to Wales, but the term 'Cytiau'r Gwyddelod' has only been used from the eighteenth century onwards.

East of Aberffraw, Anglesey, which has a natural harbour facing the hills of Ireland, a battle took place in about 470. Caswallon Lawhir (Caswallon *'long hand'*), Cunedda's grandson, led a Welsh army to final victory against the Irish near an ancient township called Cerrig y Gwyddel and the former Celtic fort of Din Dryfol, in the parish of Trefdraeth.

That, apparently, was the end of Irish settlement. Commercial and cultural connections with Ireland continued for centuries, and Wales has a shared heritage of learning, saints and legends with the Emerald Isle. Throughout the Middle Ages, Ireland was also a safe haven for many a Welsh prince on the run who would later return with Irish troops to help him regain his kingdom.

Aberffraw

Battle of Mynydd Baddon

There are two Arthurs: the historical Arthur and the Arthur of legends. Many myths are told about him, but there are very few historical facts about the man who appealed so strongly to the imagination of Europe in the Middle Ages. The roots of those facts are in Welsh culture, and in early literature, including Nennius's *Historia Brittonum* (*c.* 830). He writes that King Arthur fought twelve battles against the Saxons and defeated them every time, ensuring peace for an extended period following his last victory at Mynydd Baedon (*Mynydd Baddon* in Welsh; Latinised as *Mons Badonicus*). Gildas (a monk from the sixth century), also refers to this victory in his text and dates it to around 496.

According to Nennius, Vortigern (Gwrtheyrn in the Welsh tradition) hired soldiers from Friesland between 420 and 450 to staunch the threat from the Picts, who were attacking eastern Britain from their lands in Scotland. For their part, these mercenaries received lands near London and from this foothold expanded their territory at the expense of the Brythons (and later, the Welsh) to the west. During this first century after the departure of the Romans, Brythonic was the language spoken from Edinburgh to Cornwall. By the end of the fifth century, however, the Welsh language had evolved from this old Celtic language.

The English chronicles do not mention Arthur, but that to be expected as only Saxon victories are usually referred to! John Davies notes that the archaeological evidence points to extensive Saxon communities having spread westwards along the river Thames by 490, but halting for half a century after 500 – evidence of the strength of the Welsh under Arthur.

The picture we have of Arthur is as a leader of agile horsemen, experts in warfare. The tradition of fighting on horses is ingrained deeply in the history of the Brythons, evidenced by the need to build *chevaux de frise* (barriers to stop horses) in the line of likely attack by cavalry at Pen y Gaer, the ancient Celtic fort in the Conwy valley. The Romans had introduced new tactics to Brython horsemen and a relatively small – but quick and fierce – army would be able to deal with a much bigger Saxon army of foot soldiers only.

Nennius refers to Arthur not as *Rex* (king) but as *Dux Bellorum* (battle leader) and says an alliance of Brythonic kings appointed him as general of a united army of the kingdoms. He also states that at the battle of Mynydd Baedon Arthur shone as a leader. According to *Annales Cambriae* (Welsh Chronicles), the struggle continued for three days and three nights, and the Saxons were so completely trounced that some of them returned to their homelands on the Continent.

As with everything else associated with Arthur, the location of his twelve victories against the Saxons is the subject of much debate. However, experts can connect several of them to locations on the eastern border of Wales – Baschurch (Shropshire), Caerwent, Caerleon, Gloucester, and Leintwardine (Herefordshire).

Traditionally, historians have dated the battle at Dyrham, fought near Bath in 577, as the final geographical wedge between the Welsh and their Celtic brothers in Devon and Cornwall. But there is ample evidence that the Saxons had penetrated further west a century before that, and many of Arthur's battles were fought along the Welsh border, particularly those areas where it was relatively easy to penetrate along old Roman roads, or by sea.

Although many historians will opt for Dorset or Swindon for Arthur's final victory, Martin Hackett (referencing the work of Gilbert, Wilson and Blackett) favours a part of the Vale of Glamorgan. Before there could be a 'final victory' which would 'drive the Saxons back', they would have had to have penetrated very far

Pen y Gaer's chevaux de frise

west, isolated from reinforcements from their own territories. Roman roads and overseas links strengthen the possibility of the Vale of Glamorgan being the site, bearing in mind that Caerleon was perhaps Arthur's stronghold, and so an obvious target for enemy raids.

South of Maesteg and north of Porthcawl there is a chain of Brythonic forts on the Glamorgan Ridgeway, with numerous cairns and field names that might relate to a large war. The Bwlwarcau hill fort is presumed to be Arthur's camp and the Saxons laid siege to it for two days – an army of 1,000 horsemen could shelter within its banks and defensive ditches. It would be a plausible target for the Saxons, encamped further down, as neither its size nor defences were enormous.

On the third day, Arthur's cavalry assembled at the gate of the fort and charged at dawn towards the Saxon camp, near a hill called Mynydd Baedon. After two days of losses resulting from attacking Arthur's encampment, the Saxons' spirit was broken and many were wounded by Arthur's soldiers. Remembering what a good tactician Arthur was, it is possible that he let the Saxons venture too far, exhausting their attacking strength and then striking a lasting victory against them, ensuring that they did not pose a further risk for half a century.

Mynydd Baedon, Glamorgan Ridgeway walk near Bridgend

Battle of Camlan

Location: *Camlan farm near Dinas Mawddwy*
Battle: *Arthur/Medrawd*
Date: *about 537*

It is dangerous to try to locate events on the similarity between current names and those events. There are several geographical interpretations of the battle of Camlan, Arthur's last battle, and each depends on such speculation.

There are some facts, however, that point towards Wales being the location of this battle. Arthur was a knight with the Cross on his shield. His aim was to protect Christian lands against attacks by heathens. Enlli (*Bardsey*) was the main island of the saints in the west; it was a haven for Christian refugees (according to tradition, 900 fled there following the battle of Chester *c*. 616), a refuge for saints (20,000 are buried there), and three pilgrimages to Enlli were the equivalent of one to Rome. Moreover, it is the island of the Afallen Enlli (*Bardsey apple*). Archaeologists have discovered remains of settlements from the fifth/sixth century and as Arthur had two ships – *Prydwen* and *Gwennan* – it would be a safe retreat for his knights: far enough from the reach of Saxon ships. There is a tradition of carrying bodies to Enlli along the Cardigan Bay coast; locating Camlan in Meirionnydd is consistent with this practice.

Camlan was a battle between Brythons – even a family struggle –between Arthur and his cousin and arch-enemy, Medrawd (*Mordred*). Both were killed in that bloody battle. It does not make sense to locate it where there was friction between Brythons and Saxons. It would be far behind those lines and probably armies of only a few hundred, although the fighting is said to have been fierce and bloody, leading to huge losses on both sides. They fought until losses overwhelmed them; there was no winner.

'Camlan' can mean a meandering river, and there is a loop in the river Dyfi beside a farm called Camlan, south of Dinas Mawddwy (Grid Ref.: 852 112), with burial cairns at both ends of the battlefield. Medrawd's army would have come down from the mountains and Arthur's army up the valley, having reached Aberdyfi in

Camlan field and the Dyfi near Dinas Mawddwy

ships, maybe sailing up as far as Derwen-las. Warships at that time could hold about 120 horsemen.

It is possible that this was where the great hero was wounded. He left the Welsh with a dominance that lasted decades. A Chronicle of the English records no victory against the Brythons between 500 and 550.

Morfa Rhianedd

Location: Site of Llandudno today
Battle: Welsh (*Maelgwn Gwynedd*)/Saxons
Date: about 546

A volcanic plug forms steep hills above Deganwy and the Conwy estuary, affording naturally advantageous positions from which to protect the coast and estuary from attacks from the west. Archaeological investigations have revealed the remains of a fort from about 400 onwards, which coincides with the hypothesis that this was the stronghold of Cunedda and his family.

One of his descendants was Maelgwn, son of Caswallon, who erected a watchtower at Bodysgallen. Maelgwn built a castle on the hill and in his lifetime he secured Gwynedd as a strong kingdom. The leaders of smaller kingdoms in the north united with, and were subject to, his leadership in Deganwy. Maelgwn died of plague in 547. In addition to his military career, at his court he patronised the arts and lived luxuriously, importing wine and tableware from the eastern Mediterranean. He was also full of cunning – indeed, he might be called villainous in his demands.

There is a legend about him winning the right to be overlord over lesser kings in Wales. He called all the leaders to the coast at Aberdyfi, and they were charged with bringing their thrones with them. Remarkably, the others agreed to compete for the right to become high king by placing their grand and heavy ceremonial seats in a row on the beach as the tide came in. In facing the waves, the bravest – that is, the last to get up off his throne and flee further up the beach – would claim the title. But Maelgwn arrived with a chair made of wax and goose feathers and while the sea was up to the other kings' necks, he and his throne bobbed on the surface! Legend perhaps, but there is a stretch of sand called Maelgwn Beach at Aberdyfi to this day.

Gildas calls him *Insularis Draco* ('Dragon of the Island') acknowledging that his influence can be felt across Britain, but claims that he won his powers by killing some members of his own family. From his base in Deganwy, he created greater unity between the small kingdoms, and historians name him as 'architect of the Welsh nation'. He also aimed for cultural unity, and there is another story about him sponsoring the harp and poetry by holding a sort of eisteddfod at his court. Musicians and poets arrived, eager to compete against each other, but, privately, Maelgwn supported the men of words. At the last moment he announced that the eisteddfod would not be held in the luxurious court at Deganwy but across the river, up in the old Celtic hill fort on Conwy mountain.

There were not enough boats to take everyone, of course, and the poets and musicians had to swim across the narrow channel under the castle. By the time they reached the fort, the poets had dried out and could declaim marvellously. However, the musicians' harps were still out of tune after being soaked in estuary brine. The poets won, and it's likely that the king was well pleased. According to another anecdote, twenty-four poets accepted his patronage at the Deganwy court one Christmas.

An army of Saxons came to attack Maelgwn's fortress in Deganwy, setting up camp on Morfa Rhianedd, the dunes and marshes where Llandudno stands today. Maelgwn and his men charged from their advantageous position on the Deganwy cliffs, beating them outright. Saxon bodies lay the length and breadth of the marsh. Following the victory, the king and his men surely would have returned to Deganwy castle for more of their select Mediterranean wine.

The bodies of the enemy were left unburied. According to the *Annales*, an infection called the Yellow Plague rose from the marsh, like a yellow mist with eyes and claws.

Gildas manages to praise Maelgwn – despite his wickedness, womanising and drunkenness – for his generous sponsorship of the early saints. He gave land to establish monastic communities and churches: to Saint Deiniol at Bangor

Bodysgallen, near Llandudno

and to Saint Asaph at St. Asaph. Maelgwn fled from the Yellow Plague to another of the churches he endowed. Lest he come into contact with other people, he locked himself in Saint Eleri's church in Llanrhos. He could hear the yellow sickness moving outside the walls and his curiosity got the better of him. He ventured a look through the keyhole at the infection, and it grabbed him through the hole, through his eye, infecting his whole body, and killed him. According to one tradition, the king was buried on a nearby hill, Bryn Maelgwn (Grid Ref. 7980), but his grave is on Ynys Seiriol (*Puffin Island*) across the bay, according to another.

In 542, Yellow Plague broke out in Persia and the eastern Mediterranean then spread through Europe, especially via sea routes and ports. This was the plague that killed Maelgwn Gwynedd, according to *Buchedd Iolo* (the Iolo [Morganwg] Manuscripts), and Welsh and Brython losses are particularly severe by the end of the 540s. Despite this, it did not have much impact on the Saxons, and during the following decades they took advantage of the weakened Celts to enlarge their lands.

John Davies suggests it was the Brythons' relationship with southern Europe which brought the infection to Wales. As the Saxons did not have such links, they were not hit by the plague, he says. It seems the legend that the Yellow Plague rose from the coastal marsh is pretty accurate.

Deganwy saw several battles and many other conflicts over the centuries. Part of the castle was demolished by lightning in 810 and it was completely destroyed by the Saxons in 823. Robert of Rhuddlan, a Norman, built a wooden castle on the site in 1080 and that fell into the hands of the Welsh shortly afterwards. Llywelyn ap Iorwerth replaced it with a stone castle, but that was demolished by the English. Henry III then built a castle there in 1245, but this one was destroyed in 1263 by Llywelyn ap Gruffudd after the Welsh broke the spirit of the king's huge army and drove him back to England depleted and bereft. In 1283, Edward I used much of the stonework on the site to build his castle at Conwy, across the estuary.

Llandudno dunes below old Deganwy castle

Bangor Is-coed

It is possible that Peblig, patron saint of Llanbeblig near the Roman fort at Caernarfon, was the first recorded saint in Wales. According to tradition, Peblig (*Publicius* in Latin) was the son of Macsen Wledig (*Magnus Maximus*) and experts are certain that Christianity has been practiced there since the early fifth century, almost two hundred years before Saint Augustine was sent from Rome to England to evangelise the pagan Saxons.

During those centuries the Celtic Church developed. Its emphasis was on saints and monks, unlike the Church of Rome with its emphasis on the power of bishops. The west coast of Wales was on the 'marine highway', with saints sailing back and forth between their different churches in the Celtic countries. The Celtic Church developed closer to nature, and elements of ancient legends can be found in the faith.

The Pope sent his envoy, Saint Augustine, to convert the Saxons to Christ in 603. In Gloucestershire, Augustine met representatives from the Brythonic Church, but did not bother to stand to welcome the Welsh who, among other things, had been chastised for refusing to follow the Roman Easter. Many of them were monks at Bangor on Dee (*Bangor Is-coed*), a large monastery in the lower Dee valley. The result of the vexed meeting was for the Welsh to reject Augustine's attempt to have them evangelise the Saxons.

According to Bede, Saint Augustine threatened them by prophesying that, for refusing the Pope's request to turn them into proper Christians, the Saxons would kill them all.

At that time Aethelfrith, the pagan king of Northumbria, was defeating the provinces of the Old North one by one. From 600 to 650, he extended his kingdom to the lands of Gododdin, Elfed (Elmet, around Leeds) and Rheged (Cumbria/Lancashire), leaving Strathclyde as the only Brythonic kingdom there. Around 616, he led a powerful army towards Chester and Deeside. The Welsh, and some Cornish, united under the leadership of Selyf, king of Powys, but

The Dee bridge, Bangor on Dee

were defeated by the Northumbrians in a bloody battle near Chester – the battle of 'Bangor Orchard', according to one Welsh description. Selyf was killed, and Aethelfrith was killed in another battle soon afterwards.

From that name, it seems the battlefield was near Bangor on Dee. There was a large monastery there, with the monks spending half their time in agriculture. The course of the Dee has shifted over the centuries and some have placed the monastery at today's Bangor on Dee bridge.

Before the battle, according to Bede, twelve hundred monks from the monastery appeared on a hill above the battlefield. Aethelfrith asked what this meant, and was told that they had been fasting for three days and were there to pray for victory for the Welsh, charged to do so by Brochfael Ysgithrog, Selyf's grandfather, who had retired to the monastery.

Aethelfrith decreed that they were fighting against him with their words and ordered his troops to attack them before going on to fight against the Welsh. All but fifty of the monks are reputed to have been killed. Although the Northumbrians won the battle, their losses were large.

The battle is identified by historians as the final rift between the Welsh and the Brythons of the Old North. From then on, only Welshmen would fight the Saxons' westward advances.

To a cleric like Bede, the Augustine prophecy comes true with the slaughter of the Bangor on Dee monks. When the Welsh refused to obey the request of Saint Augustine's mission among the heathen Saxons, they could expect nothing but death by the hands of the heathen.

According to tradition, 900 refugees went to the Enlli (*Bardsey*) after losing their lands to the Northumbrians. The Maen Achwyfan Celtic cross, near Whitford in Flintshire, was erected in 1200 to remember the monks murdered at the battle of Chester.

Maen Achwyfan

Rhyd Forlas

Location: Morlas brook near Pont y Blew
Battle: Welsh/Northumbrians
Date: about 610

Stanzas in the Llywarch Hen (Llywarch *'the old'*) Cycle of poems, composed around 800 to 850, describe the defence of Rhyd Forlas (*Morlas ford*). Llywarch Hen was one of the sixth century heroes of the Old North, from the province of Rheged (the Lake District today). He lived at a time when the Northumbrian kingdom was spreading rapidly, as the Brythons were weak. In the hard-fought battles of the period, Llywarch Hen lost all but one of his twenty-four sons. Gwên ap Llywarch was the last son. To prove his gallantry to his father the lad went to protect Rhyd Forlas. That meant keeping watch all night in the wooden tower on Morlas's defensive dyke.

The ford was a weak point on their border: a place where the enemy could cross the river and attack the kingdom. Llywarch charged his son with sounding the alarm if a raid were to happen that night, to summon reserves. When the attack came Gwên did not sound the alarm. He fought and was killed, and in another series of stanzas Llywarch grieves for his brave and beloved son.

Legend and myth are the background to the poems, but they also have historical significance. We are familiar now with the picture of defending the Welsh border. After losing the battle of Chester, the Welsh would have been squeezed back westwards, beyond the Dee and gradually beyond the river Ceiriog. One of the streams flowing westwards into the Ceiriog is the Morlas and the

After leaving Chirk (Y Waun) on the old A5, and crossing the border into Shropshire, turn left at the traffic island near Weston Rhyn (signposted for St. Martin's). After about half a mile there is a narrow road to the left signposted 'Glynmorlas'. The road drops down a narrow valley and after about two miles there are a few houses and an ancient bridge over the river Ceiriog. There is parking for one car on the other side of Pont y Blew. Come back over the bridge, and a footpath runs alongside the river Ceiriog, across the field, to the Morlas brook ford (Ref. Grid 782 794). On the other side of the ford there is high earth mound where the wooden guard tower would have stood in the sixth century: Morlas Dyke.

Rhyd Forlas

Northumbrians would have had to cross it to seize more Welsh lands.

During Offa's reign as king of Mercia (757–796), the famous dyke was built. The stanzas show that fighting was already going on in the area of Offa's Dyke. The Gwên in the stanzas was defending Rhyd Forlas; today the England/Wales border still follows the part of Morlas brook where the ford lies.

Defeating the Vikings

Location: Llandudno
Battle: Welsh (Rhodri Mawr)/Vikings
Date: about 856

The first king to control almost the entire territory of the new Wales, bordered on three sides by the sea and by Offa's Dyke on the fourth, was Rhodri Mawr (Rhodri *'the great'*), who died in 878. His dynastic line included several strong kings of hard-won lands, such as Cadwaladr Fendigaid (Cadwaladr *'the blessed'*) who died in 664, whose army carried the Red Dragon, and Rhodri Molwynog (Rhodri *'the bald/white-headed'*) who died in 754. Rhodri Molwynog had won three important battle against the Anglo-Saxons, two in Radnorshire and one in Cornwall.

The border was more or less defined by the time Offa's engineering work formalised it in the eighth century. His was an earth wall, not stone like Hadrian's Wall, and there were no forts along it – although there were penalties for crossing. It was there as much to thwart Saxon ambition to steal Welsh lands as it was to prevent the Welsh rustling cattle from the Saxons. Incursions continued across the Dyke periodically – Offa himself was killed in the battle of Rhuddlan.

The Dyke assisted a Welsh identity to flourish and expand. During the years 800 to 1282 Wales experienced an exciting and inspiring time, according to John Davies: poetry and mythology flourished; powerful provinces were established and shrewd administrations developed; tribal practices were codified to create the Laws of Hywel Dda, which are still admired internationally; the churches, dioceses and abbeys became more Welsh in character; and the number of Welsh books increased.

The lesser Welsh kings were often castigated for quarrelling and fighting among themselves instead uniting to face the common enemy. Rhodri Mawr is a good example of uniting the kingdoms through marriage and discussion, according to John Davies, who notes that this practice is not uncommon. Merfyn Frych, Rhodri's father, from the Isle of Man, married Nest of Powys. In his turn, Rhodri married Angharad of Seisyllwg (a combination of Ceredigion and Ystrad Tywi – part of Carmarthenshire). Tradition has it that he met the nobility of Powys near Maen Bwlch Gwynedd on the Berwyn in 855 to inherit that province on his uncle's death. By the end of his life he ruled a kingdom that stretched from Anglesey to Gower. He was given the epithet 'Great' by the chroniclers for his contribution to consolidating the Welsh nation's political power. He established a Gwynedd royal court at Aberffraw on Anglesey and built the first castle at Dinefwr, which become the centre of Welsh power in Deheubarth, and built a court for the province of Powys, in Mathrafal. The government of Wales was organised, with meetings to resolve disputes between the provinces.

Rhodri Mawr was famous throughout western Europe as a warrior, especially for his great victory over the Vikings in 856. These warring seafarers has started attacking England from 789 onwards, killing, burning, looting, stealing people as slaves, and despoiling the treasures of monasteries and churches. They also established towns and ports to colonise and trade. By 840 their communities were well-rooted in the islands of Scotland and Ireland. From 865 onwards, the north and

The boundary stone at Bwlch Maen Gwynedd

east of England fell to the Danes, and from 911 onwards a large section of northern France was added to their territory. They were masters of the western seas.

Although Wales lies within these seas, there were no significant Viking colonies here. The shores did not provide accessible ports for their longships nor were there large, navigable rivers into the hinterland. There were also powerful kings with nimble armies that could respond quickly to threats and face them on the battlefield. In 856, Rhodri Mawr and his Welsh army faced Viking warriors and their leader, Horm, who had landed in Anglesey and ravaged the island.

The name of the Great Orme peninsula, near today's Llandudno, is associated with Horm. In the Viking language, orme means 'sea dragon' and it is record that, perhaps near Llandudno today, Rhodri defeated the Vikings. After that, Rhodri strengthened the Welsh navy to protect the shores of Traeth Mawr, near Aberffraw. The Vikings suffered a further defeat in 872, but Rhodri had to flee to Ireland temporarily after losing the day to them in 877.

Horm was killed in the battle at the foot of the Great Orme

Cymryd

Location: Conwy estuary
Battle: Welsh (Anarawd)/Mercian Army
Date: about 881

After the Welsh lost such a capable and successful leader in Rhodri Mawr, more than one army was willing to venture into the country to see how the next generation would defend itself. About 881, Aethelred, king of Mercia, and his army came to invade Gwynedd. Anarawd, Rhodri's son, was now king of Gwynedd and his brothers, Cadell and Merfyn, controlled Cardigan/Ystrad Tywi and Powys. The chronicles record the three brothers working successfully together against their enemies.

Anarawd's army faced Aethelred's army at Conwy, and the Welsh were victorious. That victory is called 'Rhodri's Revenge'.

The Mercians retreated as far as the Vale of Clwyd before returning to challenge Gwynedd on the banks of the Conwy for a second time.

This time, the battlefield was two miles up the estuary, where the river widens, and the mudflats and sandbars come and go with the tide. The Welsh faced the enemy as they crossed towards the western bank at Cymryd, near an ancient farmhouse of the same name (Ref. Grid: 793 758). This is the lowest fording point on the river; it is only possible to cross at the very lowest tides.

The ford was half a mile across, tortuous and dangerous. Because of the tidal pools on all sides, the Mercian troops could not charge forward from the rear to reinforce their army.

Gradually, the Saxons were pushed back to the ford. In time, the tide literally turned in favour of the Welsh. A vast army of Mercians was slaughtered by the swords of the Welsh, or were drowned in the river.

Looking down at Cymryd (and Llansanffraid Glan Conwy on the other side) from the west bank of the river

Rhyd-y-groes

Location: Forden (*Ffordun*)
Battle: *Welsh/Anglo-Saxons*
Date: 1039

When Gruffudd ap Llywelyn became king of Gwynedd and Powys in the 1030s, he made it clear from the outset he would not be satisfied with that territory alone. He wanted to follow Rhodri Mawr in uniting Wales into one whole country and this he managed in his lifetime, his territory encompassing the four main kingdoms. He was effective, aggressive and merciless but managed to go a step further than Rhodri ever did.

In establishing his authority over Wales, his ambition was always to weaken the threat coming from the other side of Offa's Dyke. He constantly attacked the Mercian armies and from 1055 onwards even expanded his eastern borders and won back parts of Herefordshire lost to the Welsh for generations.

Gruffudd's tactic was to defend by attacking. From his strongholds he crossed the border and destroyed Anglo-Saxon castles and towns and won several small battles before returning to his own country. In 1039, a large army was raised in Mercia to march on Wales and get revenge on Gruffudd ap Llywelyn and his forces.

The old Roman road west of Shrewsbury follows the river Camlad about five miles south of Welshpool (*Y Trallwng*). In this wooded valley a north–south Roman road crosses it at a place called Rhyd-y-groes (Grid Ref.: 201 001). In a dip here (where the caravan park is today), north of the road from Shrewsbury, Gruffudd hid his army, ready to mount a fierce surprise attack on the Anglo-Saxons.

The battlefield historian Martin Hackett paints a picture of a long line of Mercian soldiers marching along the Roman road. They would have mostly been foot soldiers carrying spears, with only Eadwine, the leader, and a select elite on horseback. The Welsh would have had the superior positioning, as they were on a ridge in the valley, with trees as cover as well.

If the Mercians had walked from

River Camlad near Rhyd-y-groes

Shrewsbury that day (which is 20 miles away), it would be late in the day by then: the marchers would be tired. It is assumed that Gruffudd's army was not very large (500/600 perhaps, as he was then not yet at his peak). By contrast, Eadwine would not have ventured over the border with fewer than about 1,000 in his army.

Gruffudd let the first Mercian troops pass by and then out of nowhere a shower of arrows, sling shots and pikes rained down on the long line of invaders. Another volley, and then Gruffudd's spearmen would come careering down the slope as the Anglo-Saxons began to deal with what was happening.

The Camlad is a small river with a bed of clay, but it has steep banks and deep pools in its meanders. When the Anglo-Saxons broke ranks, many drowned as they tried to flee across the river. Eadwine was killed and it was a total victory for Gruffudd and the Welsh – the first victory of many for Gruffudd and his army against the Saxons.

1. *The ridge and slope of the Welsh positions above the Anglo-Saxons; 2. The old Roman crossroads; 3. The battlefield between the hillside and the river*

Bron-yr-erw

Location: Bwlch Mawr near Clynnog Fawr
Battle: Gruffudd ap Cynan/Trahaearn
Date: about 1075

Once England had fallen to the Normans at the battle of Hastings in 1066, one factor the Welsh had in their favour was their habit of fighting on rugged ground. Swords, small bows, spears and axes were their normal weapons. They usually travelled and fought on foot, and defended themselves with light wooden shields and leather jerkins. These were unencumbered, agile armies.

The Normans brought different tactics to the battlefield. They favoured knights in armour – helmets like chimney pots, with a narrow nose plate; flexible chain mail; long triangular shields; and long and heavy swords. They favoured open battles on flat land. When entering enemy territory, their tactic was to create a defended encampment and, within a few days, construct a motte and bailey castle. A steep mound rising 15–30 metres was formed from the soil and stones dug out from the surrounding trench. A wooden tower was built on top of the mound, and a wooden palisade around the whole, creating a strong position in a strategic spot. By creating a chain of such castles, a large army could be serviced and protected within their enemies' land.

The Normans' feudal order led to absolute obedience to the crown. Hatred and cruelty became the hallmark of their administration. Below the king was a class of powerful barons who had free rein to extend their territories, as long as they were completely loyal to the autocratic ruler. Three mighty castles on the Welsh border were established by Hugh the Fat or Hugh the Wolf in Chester (*Huw Fras* or *Huw Flaidd* in Welsh), Roger de Montgomery in Shrewsbury, and William FitzOsbern in Hereford. Their task was to hold the border against Welsh raids and extend their grip westwards when the opportunity arose.

Wales was not united, nor was there a prominent leader, when the Normans started to penetrate the eastern lowlands.

1. An impressive motte and bailey castle in Wiston, Pembrokeshire; 2. Twthill: site of the first Norman castle in Rhuddlan

Trahaearn ap Caradog was a successful fighter in Arwystli (southern Powys), and when the Gwynedd crown became vacant he was in a strong position to grab it. At that point Gruffudd ap Cynan came from Dublin – along with an army of Irish, Danes, and Welshmen from Anglesey and Arfon – to claim that province.

His defeated father – from a dynasty of Gwynedd kings – had fled to Dublin and married Rhagnell, a Viking princess. Gruffudd was born there about 1055, and in 1075 came to Abermenai with an Irish and Viking fleet. Robert of Rhuddlan, a cunning marauder and nephew of Hugh the Wolf, had already established motte and bailey castles at Rhuddlan and Deganwy, and saw his chance to use Gruffudd to his own ends. He contributed troops and arms to the returning exile, who pressed on to Llŷn to defeat the army of Cynwrig, Trahaearn's ally. Two hundred and twenty Irish were killed, together with Gruffudd's personal host.

Trahaearn rejoiced to hear this and joined the king of Powys and men from Meirionnydd, Llŷn and Eifionydd to attack Gwynedd. They came face to face with Gruffudd's army and the rest of the Gwynedd realm at Bron-yr-erw on the eastern slopes of Bwlch Mawr, above Clynnog Fawr. It was a bloody battle with large losses on both sides. Gruffudd was in the middle of the fiercest fighting, his sword swinging back and forth, when those closest to him realised he was in mortal danger. Gwyncu, an Anglesey nobleman, grabbed him and dragged him reluctantly to a ship at Abermenai.

Gruffudd sailed back to Ireland and landed in Wexford. He had won and lost the crown of Gwynedd inside a year. But this was only the beginning for this the unrelenting fighter.

Looking down from the Bron-yr-erw battlefield to Abermenai, where Gruffudd landed with his fleet from Dublin

Mynydd Carn

Location: Garn Fawr, Dinas Cross, Pembrokeshire
Battle: Gruffudd and Rhys/Trahaearn
Date: 1081

Shortly after losing the battle of Bron-yr-erw, Gruffudd ap Cynan tried to reclaim Gwynedd once again, with an Irish and Viking fleet. He arrived at Abermenai with thirty ships; Trahaearn ap Caradog summoned supporters from Llŷn and Ardudwy to his Meirionnydd camp. In turn, Gruffudd called his supporters from Arfon and another part of Llŷn to his camp on Anglesey. It would likely be a long campaign.

This did not please the Vikings, who wanted to fight at once and get their share of the booty. When they realised there was to be no immediate battle, they set about plundering Anglesey – Gruffudd's bastion. To cap this destructive raid, Gruffudd himself was kidnapped by them and carried back to Dublin. With no army in Gwynedd, the Normans saw their chance. Hugh the Fat, Robert of Rhuddlan and other barons penetrated as far as Llŷn, killing and plundering. They were purportedly in the Llŷn Hundred for a week, leaving the countryside devastated and deserted for eight years.

Gruffudd was unable to return to Gwynedd immediately, but in 1081 he sailed from Waterford with a host of Irish, Vikings and Welsh and landed at Port Clais, near St Davids. We hear of him meeting Rhys ap Tewdwr, of the Deheubarth dynasty, there. Rhys had been exiled in Brittany for fifty years before returning to claim the Deheubarth province in 1079, but was crushed by the large armies of Trahaearn, Meilyr (Powys) and Caradog (Gwent and Glamorgan). When Gruffudd understood that he and Rhys shared the same enemies, they agreed to be allies and to march immediately to the north-east of St Davids towards the enemy camp on Mynydd Carn.

There is considerable speculation as to the battle site. The Ancient and Historical Monuments Commission for Wales proposes heathland near the Royal Air Force airfield south-west of Templeton. There used to be a large cairn – since destroyed by the air force – on the site.

The view east from Mynydd Carn

However, it is 35 km from St Davids and not mountainous. Others suggest the slopes of Carningli, above Newport on the north Pembrokeshire coast, or north of Cwm Gwaun, between the Parc y Meirw standing stones and the summit of Mynydd Llanllawer, known as Garn Fawr.

While it is tempting to see some reference to the battle graves of soldiers in the name 'Parc y Meirw' (*'field of the dead'*), those stones date back to the Bronze Age and, according to the experts, are lined up with mountains in Ireland. Yet Garn Fawr matches many elements in the story. It is a day's march from St Davids. There is level area on the east side of the mountain, suitable for an encampment. The surrounding area has 'valleys, marshes and mountains', where the enemy's troops were pursued after they broke ranks. There is an obvious 'large cairn' there which can be clearly seen on the summit, sites commonly used in the Bronze Age for heroes' burials.

Garn Fawr lies on the western spur of the mountain range to the north of the Preseli mountains. Follow the B4313 from Fishguard (*Abergwaun*) for Llanychaer, make a left turn over the bridge at Llanychaer, and go up the hill. At the first fork, turn right along a narrow road, still climbing. Within half a mile the Parc y Meirw standing stones can be seen on the right. A little further on there is a wide, flat saddle of land at the crossroads. Garn Fawr is to the left and commands spectacular scenery. Gruffudd, Rhys and their armies would have travelled all day and so the sun would have been setting behind them as they approached Garn Fawr, seeing the enemies' arms ahead glinting in the last rays. According to the story, Rhys was in favour of resting the men and waiting until the next day to fight, as night was falling.

Gruffudd's response was typical of him. Rhys could rest for twenty days if he wished, but he and his soldiers wanted to pitch themselves into the fight. And so it was, much to the surprise of his enemies. Provinces, from both east and west, head to head in a desperate skirmish in the moonlight.

Swords of the Gwynedd Welsh, double-headed Viking battleaxes, and Irish maces prevailed. The three eastern kings were killed, huge numbers of knights and soldiers were felled, and soldiers were pursued through the valleys and along the slopes all night and through the following day. Hardly any went back to their own country.

Gruffudd and Rhys were both descended from Rhodri Mawr's line and after this battle it would be these two branches of the dynasty that – until the fall of Llywelyn in 1282 – would protect the interests of Gwynedd and Deheubarth from the rapacity of the Normans. Rhys ap Tewdwr reoccupied his province later that year. He was recognised as its legitimate king by William the Conqueror on his visit to St Davids.

Gruffudd ap Cynan returned to Gwynedd, but his troubles were not over. He was tricked into meeting Robert of Rhuddlan to 'discuss peace' in Rhug, near Corwen. He and his unarmed band were pounced on by the Normans and Gruffudd seized and jailed for years in Chester castle. The first thing he did after escaping was to attack Robert and his host near Deganwy, and kill him.

Site of the Welsh castle on the Deganwy hills above the Conwy estuary

Maes Gwenllian

Location: Cwm Gwendraeth Fach
Battle: Welsh/Normans
Date: 1136

Gwenllian is one of the women who has left a deep impression on the memory and mentality of the Welsh. Armies led by women were not unusual in the Celtic tradition, and in Gwenllian's time the Laws of Hywel Dda were progressive in terms of the status of women in Welsh society. But this special story encompasses courage and grief, loss and recovery and it touches the heart.

In 1113, Gruffudd ap Rhys, king of Deheubarth, visited Gruffudd ap Cynan, king of Gwynedd, and his family at court at Aberffraw. The northern king recalled the assistance of Rhys ap Tewdwr, the southerner's father, who helped him establish himself in Gwynedd. Rhys's son was given an honourable welcome. There he met Gwenllian, daughter of the Aberffraw king, and exceptionally beautiful. They fell in love and ran away, back to Deheubarth, without her father's permission. At the time, Gruffudd ap Rhys was the leader of an army of hardened fighters who lived a rough and combative nomadic life in the forests and valleys of Deheubarth. They attacked the Norman castles at Swansea (*Abertawe*), Carmarthen (*Caerfyrddin*), Llanymddyfri and Aberystwyth and then disappeared back to the wilds. Gwenllian shared this dangerous warrior life for over twenty years, fighting at the head of the troops, shoulder to shoulder with Gruffudd.

When Henry I died in 1135, there were disputes between the Norman barons; Gruffudd and Gwenllian saw their chance to strike. Hywel ap Meredith of Breconshire (*Brycheiniog*) had won a crucial victory against the Normans of Gower at the battle of Garn Goch near Loughor (*Llwchwr*) on New Year's Day 1136, in which the horses were said to have been up to their fetlocks in blood. Gruffudd ap Rhys decided to take his eldest and youngest sons with him to see his father-in-law in Aberffraw to try to persuade him join the raids against the Normans. He left his two middle sons, Maelgwn and Morgan, with Gwenllian and

1. Battle of Garn Goch memorial;
2. Kidwelly Castle

his army in the Caio (*Caeo*) area, in the forests of northern Carmarthenshire.

While Gruffudd was in the north, Maurice de Londres led some of the other Norman barons in fierce raids against Deheubarth. Gwenllian knew the Welsh could not avoid a set battle for long, and summoned her captains. Most of the best men had gone to escort Gruffudd, but the rest of the army was loyal to her. News reached her that Maurice's numerous troops had landed near Kidwelly castle, and Gwenllian knew she had no choice now but to lead the Deheubarth army against them.

Many ordinary Carmarthenshire country folk joined her as she and Maelgwn (18) and Morgan (16) led the way down to Cwm Gwendraeth Fach. On approaching Kidwelly's meadows, they could see the Norman camp and realised that their army was far greater than Deheubarth's. Martin Hackett suggests that the Welsh camped on the steep slopes to the east of Maes Gwenllian, under Glanhiraeth ridge, near Mynyddygarreg.

The battle resulted in a tragic loss for the Deheubarth Welsh – they did not have the weapons, experience or numbers of the Normans. But they had Gwenllian and her sons to lead them and, so the story goes, the three of them did their utmost bravely. Hundreds of Welshmen were killed, including Maelgwn, and tradition has it that the Normans captured and decapitated Gwenllian after the battle. All were buried in a mass grave on Maes Gwenllian. Morgan was also caught and killed in front of his mother on the battlefield.

Gwenllian's courage and her treatment by the Normans outraged the Welsh and certainly stiffened their resolve. The Welsh flocked to the armies of her husband and brothers and this was the beginning of a period of hitting back, winning victory after victory. The war cry of the Welsh in these battles, legend has it, was 'Gwenllian!'

Gwenllian farm from Mynyddygarreg and Gwenllian's battlefield on the right, with Kidwelly Castle in the distance

Crug Mawr

Location: North of Cardigan; Grid Ref.: 206,474
Battle: Welsh/Normans
Date: 1136

In April 1136, the Welshmen of Gwent attacked Richard FitzGilbert, the lord of Ceredigion, and his convoy, in Coed Grwyne above Crickhowell (*Crugywel*). He was killed.

Here, perhaps, was one of the first instances of a new weapon being used by the Welsh, a weapon that would revolutionise battle tactics in Europe over the following centuries. That weapon was the Welsh longbow, and it was invented and first used in south Wales. For centuries, the 'small bow' was adequate against soldiers wearing no more than leather jerkins for protection. But when the Norman cavalry with their armour, and infantry with their chain mail, arrived a longer and thicker bow was needed to power the arrows through the protective chain mail.

The solution, created in Gwent and Glamorgan, was a bow the height of a man, six feet long. An experienced bowman could fire 15 arrows a minute, until the sky was thick with them. A longbow's arrow could wound a soldier at 150 metres and up to about 50 metres could drive through armour and flesh up to the shaft. In 1188, according to Gerallt Gymro (*'Gerallt of Wales'*), Welsh arrowheads were found to have penetrated an oak door four inches thick during the siege of Abergavenny (*Y Fenni*) castle. Gerallt noted that the Gwent and Glamorgan archers were the best, and that the Normans dreaded them. When Welsh chiefs met with William de Brensa in Abergavenny castle, the Norman insisted that they swear that none of their followers would carry a longbow ever again!

Although much is made of the 'English Longbow' by some of England's imperial historians, nobody denies that the Welsh invention to defend their country and their freedom was what the weapon originally was. Horsemen in heavy armour, trying to occupy the forests and valleys of Wales, fell to the longbow. Neither plate iron armour nor thick chain mail could withstand the blow of longbow arrows.

Although bows are common on several

Crug Mawr and the battlefield near Cardigan

continents, a particularly strong bow was developed in the valleys of Gwent, Glamorgan and the Tywi. The heartwood from an elm or a yew trunk which had grown in a rough and shady location would be used, so the tree would have developed slowly with a close and strong grain.

Archery was part of the education and accomplishment of all boys as they grew up. It had developed from the art of hunting, of course, and even when daily hunting to eat was no longer a necessity, the practice of hunting continued as a very popular recreational activity in Wales in the Middle Ages. Archery was practised daily, with shooting competitions after church service on Sundays.

According to the evidence, short, weak bows were used by both sides during the battle of Hastings in 1066. Welsh soldiers were lightly armed for fast movement and surprise attacks. These bows were particularly effective for this method of warfare. The Norman knights had no hope of defeating the armies of the Welsh on their own ground – the only effective tactic was to divide the Welsh principalities and use the archers from defeated regions in the east to attack the western, independent armies.

FitzGilbert was cornered in Coed Grwyne by a host of 'excellent Gwent archers' under the leadership of Morgan ap Owain. The Norman and his whole convoy were killed in a hail of arrows. There now existed a soldier on foot, in lightweight leather, who could challenge and defeat professional knights.

The Welsh continued their attacks on the Normans in retribution for their treatment of the princess Gwenllian. A Gwynedd army, led by Gwenllian's brothers Owain and Cadwaladr, crossed the river Dyfi, and razed five Norman castles in Ceredigion on their way to the south of the county.

By the autumn, Owain and Cadwaladr, along with the Deheubarth army under the leadership of Gruffudd ap Rhys, and forces from mid-Wales, had gathered north of Cardigan (*Aberteifi*). Their number included heavily-armoured cavalry and also regiments of foot soldiers clad in chain mail. These were no hit and run soldiers in the guerrilla tradition. This time the Welsh were on a national campaign, ready to fight on open fields and

Norman castle at Aberystwyth

with no intention of turning tail. The spoil stolen from the Norman castles was put to good use.

It is believed that an army of about 3,000 from all over south Wales had been mustered in Cardigan by the Normans, including about 500 cavalrymen. It marched northwards from Cardigan, and the striking hills around Crug Mawr afforded ideal hiding places for the Welsh forces. The record shows that the Welsh divided themselves into three organised, military sections. Maybe one faction took the gap facing the town and the rest hid either side of a hillock, shaped like an inverted funnel. Once the battle began, two sections closed round the Norman army in a pincer movement. In the biggest battle on Welsh soil since the Norman conquest of England, the Normans turned and fled for the town. Some managed to reach the castle, but the others had to throw themselves into the river Teifi and many drowned. The town was burned to the ground.

This was a tremendous victory following a successful campaign through Ceredigion. After that, the political map of south Wales changed totally as the Welsh reclaimed their lands and castles. Carmarthen and nearby castles fell into their hands in 1137 and the old warrior Gruffudd ap Cynan, by then in his eighties, came all the way from Aberffraw to Ystrad Tywi to celebrate these victories.

By 1146 Rhys, youngest son of Gruffudd and Gwenllian, joined the raid to seize Llansteffan castle. The success of the Welsh of Deheubarth would continue under his leadership over the following decades. By the time he was the Lord Rhys he attacked and burned Kidwelly castle and proceeded to hound the Normans out of Cardigan and build his own stone castle there. This was the first stone castle to be built by a Welsh prince.

Cardigan castle

Crogen

Location: Ceiriog valley
Battle: Welsh (Owain Gwynedd)/English
Date: 1165

Owain Gwynedd's father, Gruffudd ap Cynan, had to re-establish his claim over the kingdom Gwynedd more than once in his lifetime. Soon after his Mynydd Carn victory, he was betrayed by Meirion Goch – one of his own captains – into the hands of Robert of Rhuddlan. He spent twelve years as a captive of the Normans, the last ones in Chester castle's prison, infamous for being the most vicious jail of all. Released from there in a daring raid by Cynwrig Hir (Cynwrig 'the tall') and his comrades, he took care not to be betrayed again. He created a tight regiment of about 160 totally faithful men, who were family, he could expand his army as required by calling on allies from neighbouring kingdoms. He strengthened his connections by marriage and by getting rid of his enemies, and by 1099 he had released Gwynedd from the Norman grip.

By 1124, Gruffudd's sons – Cadwallon, Owain and Cadwaladr – were old and experienced enough to help him expand his territory. He transferred his resolve and aspirations to the next generation.

Of those sons, Owain grew into an influential and successful leader, in Gwynedd and throughout Wales. He added Meirionnydd and Ceredigion to his kingdom, and by 1146 he had restored the eastern border as far as the Dee near Chester. When Henry II came to the English throne in 1154, Gwynedd was stronger and larger under Owain than was before the Normans arrived. Although Henry II attacked Wales four times between 1157 and 1165, and with significant resources and armies at that, he failed in his ambition to conquer and occupy the country. Henry II was the first king of England who tried conquering all of Wales, and the fact that the Welsh prevailed is a tribute to the military and political capability of Owain Gwynedd.

Henry II had a huge empire behind him – the British Isles and most of France. Owain's strength was that he and his fellow Welshmen had an independent spirit which proved indomitable. He

1. Pont Melin y Castell near Crogen; 2. Plaque on the bridge; 3. Woods along the river Ceiriog

THIS PLAQUE COMMEMORATES

MAE'R PLAC HWN I GOFFAU

THIS BATTLE WAS PART
OF THE BERFA MOUNTAINS
CAMPAIGN. WALES FOUGHT FOR ITS
FREEDOM FROM ENGLISH DOMINATION

OWAIN GWYNEDD   GRUFFUDD MAELOR   HENRY II

THE BATTLE of CROGEN

YMA'R GODD BRWYDR CROGEN RHWNG BYDDIN
HENRI II BRENIN LLOEGR A BYDDIN CYMRU DAN
ARWEINIAD OWAIN GWYNEDD

NEARBY IN AUGUST 1165 A BLOODY BATTLE WAS FOUGHT
BETWEEN HENRY II, KING OF ENGLAND (1133-1189) AND
WELSH FORCES UNDER OWAIN GWYNEDD (1137-70)

PLAC WEDI EI DDADORCHUDDIO GAN
FUNDED BY CADBURY'S CHIRK AND UNVEILED BY
4 MARCH 2009

managed to overcome minor squabbles that divided and sapped his fellow leaders and forge them into one corps with a shared vision.

Owain defeated the first English incursion near Basingwerk on Wales's north-east coast. As early as this, it was clear that the Welsh identification with their land and country was as crucial as Henry II's lack of recognition of it. Henry was lucky not to be killed himself during the trouncing his army received. Shortly afterwards came the news that the king of England's navy, sent to decimate Anglesey, was beached with some of the ships torched and the troops defeated by the men of the island in the battle of Tal-y-moelfre.

After his first failure, Henry II went on to build and strengthen his castles in the north-east, but Owain was far-sighted enough to wait for his chance. The English king tried to squeeze the Welsh princes further and get them to give up their independence completely and bow to the authority of the crown in London.

That had the effect of uniting the Welsh, with Owain as leader. With a new determination to free themselves from Norman shackles, the Lord Rhys of Deheubarth attacked the enemy's castles in Ceredigion in 1164 while Gwynedd's army attacked those in the north-east. In a fury, Henry II prepared a force to conquer the Welsh once and for all. In Shrewsbury he assembled 5,000–6,000 troops to invade Wales. Rather than follow the old Roman road along the north coast, he chose a route up the Ceiriog valley.

To face this huge invading army, armies from Powys, Gwynedd and Deheubarth came together in early summer 1165 at Caer Drewyn, an old Brythonic hill fort near Corwen. This was later known as the 'One Wales' army – and it is estimated that it comprised about 2,000 soldiers. As ever, the Welsh tactic was to strike and harry, using the lie of their land and stones and trees to their advantage. Never was this used more effectively in our history than at the battle Crogen – the 'battle in the woods'.

Up the Ceiriog valley on the B4500 from Chirk (*Y Waun*) there are steep, wooded slopes pressing in on narrow meadows. Below the village of Bron-y-garth there is a plaque on the bridge commemorating the battle of Crogen and there are houses called Crogen Iddon and Crogen Wladys on the slopes higher up the valley. Here, in the shadow of Offa's Dyke itself, rank upon rank of the Owain Gwynedd's soldiers threw themselves into the fray. The fighting was so fierce, so determined and so unyielding over many days and nights that after that the slang word in the English army for 'courage/heart' was 'crogen'.

The narrow and wooded ground was not suitable for the movement of a large army. With troops in single file on a narrow path by the swift river, the Welshmen start battering them, their advances rapid and bloody, and then falling back for others to fill the ranks. It was a fight at close quarters, face to face, and there was no way to escape major losses on both sides. But the Welsh were not going to surrender the land. Henry II sent for foresters from Shrewsbury to clear a path in front of his army but they too were swept aside by the ferocity of Owain's men. In the end, the English were forced to the uplands, above the tree line.

On the Berwyn mountains, the attackers faced other problems – peat bogs and stormy weather without shelter and the Welsh attacking their trucks and stealing their weapons, tents, and food. Mid-August whirlwinds raged and hail pounded on the Berwyn tops. This route is called 'Ffordd y Saeson' (*the 'English road'*) to this day. With his troops dying of cold and hunger, Henry had to turn back for England under a cloud of defeat. He did not return to Wales.

His only means of retribution was to take his revenge on twenty-two sons of Welsh noblemen, held as hostages in his prisons. He killed some and put others' eyes out with hot irons, including Rhys and Cadwallon, Owain's sons.

Having withstood the full force of the Norman empire and gained the upper hand in the battle, Owain went on to further victories. He captured and burned Basingwerk castle in 1166 and Rhuddlan and Prestatyn castles in 1167. By 1168, he was at his peak as a prince, and his kingdom extended to the gates of Chester.

Abermule (Abermiwl)

Location: West of Montgomery castle
Battle: Welsh (Llywelyn Fawr)/Normans
Date: 1231

Llywelyn ap Iorwerth (*c.* 1173–1240), prince of Gwynedd, lost his father at an early age. Aged about twelve, he began his career as a warrior. His first task was fighting civil wars against his uncles and cousins to gain control over the kingdom of Gwynedd. He succeeded by 1199. It was clear from these early days that he had the same vision as his grandfather, Owain Gwynedd: to unite all of Wales under his protection. He went on to occupy Powys and Ceredigion, simultaneously maintaining King John of England's royal favour. John gave Llywelyn his daughter, Joan (*Siwan*, in Welsh), as his wife and an important manor house in Ellesmere, Shropshire.

But by 1211 relations between Llywelyn and the king had soured: John attacked Gwynedd twice and forced Llywelyn to accept harsh terms. Gradually, Llywelyn regained his lands. He sided with some of the mighty English barons who forced John to sign Magna Carta in 1215. In an assembly of all the princes of Wales in Aberdyfi in 1216, he established his authority over the whole country. It's no wonder he is known as Llywelyn Fawr (Llywelyn *'the great'*).

In 1216 the throne of England passed from John to Henry III, a boy of only nine. There was a period of instability and Llywelyn saw three military campaigns by the English crown in Wales, in 1223, 1228 and 1231. Through struggle and his children's political marriages, cunning alliances and negotiating wisely, Llywelyn kept his lands and his support among the other princes of Wales on the whole, and one military victory in 1231 was key to his career.

In April 1231, Llywelyn's armies attacked some of the Marcher barons' lands in the Montgomery (*Trefaldwyn*) area and the powerful landowner Hubert de Burgh sent a large army to Montgomery castle to try and control the Welsh. In one raid, de Burgh and his troops managed to surround a regiment of Llywelyn's soldiers and brought their captives to Montgomery. There, their heads were cut off and send to the king in London.

Montgomery castle

Naturally, this massacre enraged Llywelyn. He waged war against the Norman castles, capturing and burning a series of them in Powys and south-east Wales. He approached Montgomery castle, camping in the marshland west of the town, but the king sent a strong army to reinforce the castle garrison.

With the enemy all within the castle walls, Llywelyn sent a monk from Llanilltud to the town and he 'happened' to mention that Llywelyn himself and a few hundred of his soldiers had been seen south of the Severn, and therefore on the same side of the river as Montgomery. The significance of this to the garrison was that they feared an attack from the hills behind them rather than via the ford below the castle, which was much easier to defend. But the bait in the monk's story was that Llywelyn and his men were on the Severn floodplain, where Welsh defence would be difficult.

Immediately de Burgh ordered his army to arm and ride out of Montgomery westward towards Llandysul and Kerry (*Ceri*), along the crest of the hills. They saw a Welsh troop, who fled for the cover of a wood when they saw the riders approaching. But this was all a trap, of course. The Normans charged full speed into the marshy woodland and straight into the Welsh arrows and spears. It was a tough battle, but the Welsh were victorious. In the meantime, the bulk of Llywelyn's army had taken the opportunity to sack Montgomery.

The king's army was forced to leave Wales empty handed again. By 1234, Llywelyn had negotiated favourable peace terms with the king of England. There was no further attack by the crown on Llywelyn's lands until his death in 1240.

The Montgomery garrison's army were lured to this dip near Abermule, caught in a Welsh trap and beaten on marshy and unfamiliar ground

Deganwy

Location: Both sides of the river Conwy
Battle: Welsh (Dafydd ap Llywelyn)/English
Date: 1245

Llywelyn was succeeded by his son, Dafydd. Although Henry III had recognised Dafydd's rights as heir, when Llywelyn died a huge army led by the king of England attacked Wales. During the following years, until Dafydd's death by illness in 1246, continuous battling wore down Welsh resistance to almost nothing.

In 1244 unity among the Welsh was restored and an alliance of princes attacked the English, capturing Mold castle. In August that year, Henry III invaded north Wales yet again, leading an army along the coast. He reached as far as Deganwy, where he encountered Dafydd and the Welsh army in the passes between the hills. It was a great victory for the Welsh.

But the English did not retreat back across Offa's Dyke. It was a vexed autumn and winter, with Henry and his army camped in the Deganwy area for ten weeks and Dafydd and the Welsh army opposite, on the Conwy coastal marsh. By night, there would be swift, covert attacks across the narrow estuary mouth, the low tide revealing English bodies on poles.

A letter from the cleric Matthew Paris records low morale in the king of England's camp: in their tents they were suffering from hunger, cold and fear of the Welsh. At the end of September, we hear of a ship from Ireland reaching the narrow estuary, laden with food and wine to assuage the needs of Henry's army. She was accidentally landed on the western, Conwy shore and as the sea was ebbing, was soon beached. The Welsh rushed to raid her cargo, but the Normans sent three hundred soldiers over the estuary in boats. The Welsh retreated to the woods and mountains with Henry's soldiers in pursuit, who killed several of the Welsh and stopped at Aberconwy abbey on their way back, stealing all its contents, including the library and the communion vessels, and burning the place. That angered the Welsh and spurred them back into battle to repossess the spoils. One hundred of the three hundred English were killed, or taken prisoner and executed, and others drowned in the estuary while trying to flee. The ship fell to

the Welsh, who emptied and torched it.

Gradually the resources and food of Henry and his army became scarce as they tried to reinforce the old castle to defend themselves against the Welsh. The constant raids undermined confidence and, by winter, hunger and cold claimed lives. He had to return to England under the terms of a Welsh truce.

Narrow part of the estuary under Deganwy castle

Coed Llathen

Location: Near the Tywi/Cothi confluence
Battle: Welsh (Llywelyn ap Gruffudd)/English
Date: 2 June, 1257

In the turbulent years following the death of the young Dafydd ap Llywelyn, Llywelyn Fawr's grandson – Llywelyn ap Gruffudd – appeared as a shrewd leader and capable soldier. He defeated his older brothers to secure his hold on Gwynedd, and by 1257 the Deheubarth princes supported him.

But Rhys Fychan, a distant relation of Llywelyn, was collecting onerous taxes in the Tywi valley for the king. Llywelyn supplanted him at Dinefwr castle, continuing his campaign against the Normans along the borders of his principality. Stephen Bauzan was the Carmarthenshire county sheriff and it was his duty to restore Rhys Fychan to his post and assist him to collect taxes allegedly owing by stealing and looting. He assembled a large army in Carmarthen (*Caerfyrddin*) and travelled up the Tywi valley towards Llandeilo. It is estimated that he had about 4,000 men: foot soldiers and number of knights as well.

The Normans camped on the valley meadows, a little way off from Dinefwr castle. Rhys Fychan then played a dangerous game – until then, he had been part of the Norman army. Fearful of being caught and suffering a horrendous traitor's punishment, he left the camp, went to Dinefwr castle and declared his loyalty to Maredudd ap Rhys.

Although the Welsh did not have as many troops as the Normans, their tactics more than made up for it. From the cover of trees and rocks, their bowmen loosed arrows into the midst of the enemy camp. The Normans endured these attacks for some time and then decided it would be safer to return to Carmarthen.

It was a slow journey, during a long midsummer day. Wherever the army filed through woods and along slopes within reach of the Welsh shots, they lost men. The main battle took place in a place called Coed Llathen, the second word probably being a compression of 'Llangathen'. There, the road runs for two miles under overhanging steep slopes. The Welsh attacked at noon, in full midday

1. Pont ar Gothi; 2. Ford on the Cothi; 3. The battlefield prior to the Normans being driven into the river

sun, when the foreign army had already marched six miles. First came arrows and pikes, followed downhill by soldiers bearing long spears to unseat the horsemen. The Welsh stole their packhorses and all their reserve equipment and weapons.

The leading Norman troops fled down the valley but they were still more than ten miles from Carmarthen. As they tried to cross the river Cothi along a narrow wooden bridge, Welsh arrows rained down on their heads. The spearmen closed in behind them and there was a massacre on the river meadows near the Cothi and Tywi confluence.

The Coed Llathen/Cymerau battle was one of flight and pursuit over two days, and almost two thousand Normans were killed, including barons and noblemen. Llywelyn and his army went on to defeat the invaders in Llansteffan, Maenclochog and Narberth (*Arberth*) castles, returning to Gwynedd with huge spoils.

The entrance to Hawarden castle park can be difficult to detect even today. From the cross in the centre of the village, gate posts and a large closed door can be seen. In the large door there is a small door, but that seems equally unwelcoming and private. Yet, once opened, there is pleasant parkland with inviting paths. A mound and stone tower soon come into view. Here, by night, Dafydd and his host made a strike for independence in 1282.

Hawarden

Location: Hawarden castle
Battle: Welsh (*Dafydd ap Gruffudd*)/Normans
Date: *Palm Sunday, 22 March, 1282*

By 1258 Llywelyn ap Gruffudd had demanded the allegiance of all the lesser princes in Wales. His ambition was to establish an independent Wales, with its own government and laws. He sided with Simon de Montfort during the war in 1264 between the Marcher barons and Henry III. Llywelyn conquered castles loyal to Henry on the border, and a strong cohort of Welshmen fought in de Montfort's army. They had initial success, defeating and capturing Henry and his son Edward. But Edward managed to escape and led an army to victory against de Montfort at Evesham in 1265.

In September 1267, Llywelyn and Henry met near Rhyd Chwima ('*Ford of Rhydwhyman*') near Montgomery (*Trefaldwyn*). In their treaty Llywelyn was recognised as Prince of Wales. Hereditary rights were granted to Llywelyn as crown. There was a special constitutional significance to this agreement – the hope of creating a Welsh state was on the brink of being realised.

But there was a price to pay: heavy taxes were imposed on Wales – taxes that were impossible for Llywelyn to pay. Edward was crowned king of England in 1272 and demanded that Llywelyn meet him to swear allegiance at Shrewsbury and then at Chester, but Llywelyn considered it wiser to keep his distance. In 1277, Edward attacked north Wales, sending a fleet to invade Anglesey at the same time.

'Môn, mam Cymru' ('*Anglesey, mother of Wales*'), is the old saying about where Gwynedd sourced its grain. With the English occupying his granary, Llywelyn

had to surrender and sign the Treaty of Aberconwy, which severely curtailed the rights of the Welsh.

Until then, Dafydd ap Gruffudd, Llywelyn's brother, had been something of a turncoat. He had sided against his brother with Edward, although at times he had also been on the side of the Welsh. Under the terms of the 1277 treaty, the land between Conwy and Chester was put into Dafydd's hands but, unexpectedly, the attack that led to the Second War of Welsh Independence against Edward came from this quarter in 1282.

Edward was trying to enforce the law of England on Wales and Dafydd had forfeited his children as ransom to the English at the Chester court. The Marcher Welsh supported Dafydd, who reconciled with his brother and attacked Hawarden (*Penarlâg*) castle.

It was a night-time raid, on Palm Sunday, 1282. The garrison was killed and Roger de Clifford, magistrate and chief administrator of English law in Wales, was taken prisoner. An army from Penllyn and Powys attacked Oswestry and three days later Aberystwyth castle fell to the Ceredigion Welsh. At the same time, the Ystrad Tywi Welsh attacked Llanymddyfri and Carreg Cennen castles. It was clear that a nationally organised conspiracy was behind these. Dafydd sparked the rebellion, but within a few weeks Llywelyn was also in the midst of the attacks on English towns and castles in Wales.

Simultaneously, other Welsh armies went to capture Flint and Rhuddlan castles, and plundered both boroughs, the only two colonies in north Wales in the possession of the English by then.

1. *Hawarden castle;*
2. *Rhyd Chwima* (*Rhydwhyman*)*on the Severn*

Moel-y-don

Location: Menai Strait near Felinheli
Battle: Welsh/English
Date: 6 November, 1282

At first the Welsh were successful in the 1282 War of Independence. Clearly, the repressive English governance was not popular among the various kingdoms and the Welsh people rose with Llywelyn and Dafydd against the alien castles and towns. But by the summer, after securing loans from banks in Lucca, Firenze and Siena, Edward I had gathered massive feudal armies from all over England, as well as mercenaries from the Continent. Anglesey (*Môn*) fell to an attack by a fleet from Chester; between Conwy and Chester the country fell into the hands of one of the most powerful imperial armies ever seen.

Then, in June, Llywelyn suffered a huge personal loss when Eleanor, his wife, died at the birth of their first child, Gwenllian. Any attempt to negotiate a settlement with Edward was futile. It was clear that the king of England had set his sights on completely beating the Welsh, eliminating the authority of the princes, and occupying the land.

Gradually, Edward's armies recaptured the Norman castles, but with winter closing in, mainland Gwynedd Uwch Conwy was still standing firm. This was the mountain heartland, with strategic castles protecting all passes and valleys. Moreover, the broad Conwy estuary protected the eastern border of Snowdonia (*Eryri*) and the tides and currents of the Menai Strait, the northern border.

Mindful of this, the English decided to construct a pontoon bridge made of boats so the army could cross from Anglesey to the mainland and challenge the Welsh mountain strongholds. From late May 1282, there were a dozen carpenters preparing boats in Chester. By November, the boats were all on Anglesey and coupled to each other, creating a wooden pontoon across the Strait.

Although Edward had a substantial

1. Pleasure boats in the Strait under the slopes of Felinheli today; 2. On the Anglesey shore are wharf remains from the old ferry which carried passengers and goods for centuries from Moel-y-don. Here the English erected their pontoon bridge in the middle of winter.

army on Anglesey, he aimed to move his army in north-east Wales to cross the river Conwy and attack Snowdonia simultaneously. He planned to cross at a ford in the Llanrwst area, but had serious problems in the wooded valleys and rugged moorland between the rivers Clwyd and Conwy.

Before Edward and his army crossed the Conwy, his knights on Anglesey decided that it was time to cross the Strait on the pontoon at Moel-y-don, opposite Felinheli. Several knights and three hundred foot soldiers did this on 6 November, at low tide. After landing and forming up on slightly higher land, the tide rose and was too deep for them to get back to the bridge. The Welsh attacked them from the mountains and it was clear from the outset that the English had no hope of winning. Some tried to get back on the bridge, but their armour was so heavy they drowned. Edward lost some of his best soldiers and knights that day and it was almost the tipping point towards failure in his efforts to defeat the Welsh.

Pont Orewyn

Location: River Irfon near Builth Wells
Battle: Welsh/English
Date: 11 December, 1282

Following the rout on the Menai shore and with Edward and his army confined to Rhuddlan by the Conwy's winter flow, it seemed the stronghold of Welsh independence in the Snowdonia (*Eryri*) mountains was safe for a while. But then came a twist in the tale. Llywelyn left Snowdonia in his brother Dafydd's care and ventured towards mid-Wales with half his army. There, dramatic events took place that affected the history of Wales for centuries thereafter.

The chronicles suggest that Llywelyn was duped into leaving Gwynedd, to further the rebellion the Buellt area of Breconshire, by some of his own advisers. He may have received fraudulent promises of support by the Mortimer family, Normans of Builth Wells (*Llanfair-ym-Muallt*). Historians still argue over the details, but it seems that a trap was set to eliminate the biggest threat to the English crown: Llywelyn ap Gruffudd himself.

It is recorded that the Prince of Wales was killed, under suspicious circumstances, by an English knight while separated from his army on the bank of the river Irfon. His head was later sent to Edward at Rhuddlan; he arranged that it be paraded through the streets of London on a pole before being exhibited at the Tower of London. Monks from the Cistercian abbey at Cwmhir took Llywelyn's remains to buried there, where a memorial stone may now be seen.

On the fateful day, Llywelyn's army was on a tongue of land between the rivers Wye and Irfon, west of their confluence near Builth. With the mountains behind, they faced the king's large mid-Wales army on the other side of the Irfon, led by Roger Lestrange. Llywelyn had set guards to protect the bridge over the river Irfon – Pont Orewyn, just west of the existing bridge, perhaps at Cilmeri.

The English were advised to cross using a nearby ford and to attack the Pont Orewyn guard from behind. According to

1. Pont Orewyn as it is today over the Irfon ford near the town; 2. Cilmeri; 3. The well in which, according to tradition, Llywelyn's head was washed

1

2

GER Y FAN HON
Y LLADDWYD
LLYWELYN
EIN LLYW OLAF
1282

3

legend, Lestrange had a regiment of Gwent longbow men among the horses. A volley of arrows hit the bridge guards and it was then an easy task for the cavalry to clear the bridge. Perhaps that was the moment that Llywelyn left his army and galloped to see what was going on at Pont Orewyn, thereby being run through by the spear by one of the knights at Cilmeri. The bridge was now open for the main body of the English army to cross the river and carry out an unexpected attack on the Welsh army, carrying the day in a bloody skirmish.

With the news that the Welsh army was vanquished and Llywelyn killed there would have been joy and celebration around Edward's tables at Rhuddlan. Feelings of a national grief, and consciousness of the tragedy and devastation are expressed in the memorial odes to the Prince of Wales by Welsh bards.

Llywelyn ap Gruffudd monument in Cilmeri

Caernarfon Castle

Location: Caernarfon town and castle
Battle: Welsh (Madog ap Llywelyn)/English
Date: 1294

After Llywelyn was killed at Cilmeri he was succeeded by his brother, Dafydd. Early in 1283, Edward's armies crossed the river Conwy and captured Dolwyddelan castle for the first time ever. Dafydd and his garrison had to leave his Abergwyngregyn court and seek refuge in remote Snowdonian (*Eryri*) valleys. There he was captured in June 1283 and executed in Shrewsbury in early October by being dragged, tied to horses' tails, then hung, drawn and quartered.

Edward followed the Roman pattern by securing an 'iron ring' of strong, strategic points across north Wales. Between 1276 and 1295, he ordered the erection or repair of seventeen castles. He established privileged boroughs for the foreigners in the shadow of most of the castles, while eliminating the courts and princes of the Welsh. As a result of this, the country was now a colony: her indigenous people had no rights and English rule involved raising taxes and forcing men to fight their wars in other parts of the kingdom.

In 1287, Rhys ap Maredudd rose in rebellion and attacked the property of Englishmen in the Tywi valley. He was forced to retreat to the hills, but managed to continue his guerrilla fight for another four years before being captured and executed in 1292.

The last major challenger to Edward's authority in Wales was Madog ap Llywelyn; one of a dynasty of Gwynedd princes. His was a short-lived rebellion, over within ten months, but it was serious enough to endanger the life of Edward himself during an intense siege of Conwy castle.

The English authorities insisted on heavier taxes and more soldiers for their armies from Wales. Edward was at war in France and the colony of Wales was obliged to contribute. Welsh soldiers revolted and remained at home in Anglesey (*Môn*), Arfon and Meirionnydd. On the other hand, the Shropshire and Cheshire regiments – the very ones that would be sent to quell any disorder in Wales – had gone to Portsmouth and were about to leave for France. Because of this, Edward's garrisons in his Welsh castles were depleted.

This was a good opportunity, and one that Madog took advantage of. Anglesey experienced the first flames, in September 1294, at Michaelmas. English property at Llanfaes was attacked – there were no castles on Anglesey at the time, because Beaumaris castle was only built after this uprising. Other parts of the island were pillaged before the rebels crossed the Strait and attacked the town and castle of Caernarfon, bastion of English power and the location of the exchequer in north Wales.

The invasion was so rapid that the English town had not heard of the attacks on the Anglesey colonists. It was fair day in Caernarfon and there were a number of Welsh people from outside the walls there, as well as the 300 to 400 Englishmen planted there by Edward in the privileged colony. According to the town charter of 1284, it was compulsory for all residents living within eight miles of the town to come to the market to buy and sell all goods there at prices set by the English townsfolk.

Caernarfon Castle was the masterpiece of Edward's architects, with an imperial tone to its design and purpose. It was a statement and a celebration of the power of the English crown. That is what made

Madog's uprising such an achievement: not only did he manage to capture and burn the town, but also occupy and totally subjugate the castle itself. This would be the only time in its history that Caernarfon castle fell to the 'enemy'.

Because of Edward's multiple wars, the demand for substantial military and financial resources continued. His grand plan to erect castles and walled towns in Wales brought him close to bankruptcy – this was the largest construction project seen in Europe during the Middle Ages. Faced with those costs and the crown's financial difficulties, the work on the Caernarfon walls had slowed, and even delayed, by 1292. A wooden palisade closed the gap in the wall on the north side of the town.

That is the side facing the Strait and Anglesey. Madog and his men attacked the town from that direction and mercilessly slaughtered the colonists. It had a lasting impact on the town – there was a shortage of volunteers to colonise Caernarfon afterwards, and extraordinary privileges were granted to try and attract them.

The crown's buildings were burned; the mill demolished; the town walls breached; the quay burned; and the exchequer was attacked, the money stolen and documents burned, including the town charter. The castle fell into the hands of the rebels. The Anglesey sheriff, Roger de Puleston, was caught and hanged by two of his tenants.

Simultaneously in other parts of Wales, other leaders of the rebellion captured Cardigan (*Aberteifi*) castle, executed crown officials in mid-Wales and attacked Caerphilly castle. In no time, many of the castles of the English in Wales were besieged and Madog and his followers triumphed against Henry de Lacy's army near Denbigh (*Dinbych*).

When the news reached Edward, he gave up his plans to go to war in France. He led an army to north Wales, said to be 30,000 strong. When he could not cross back over the flooded Conwy, he was besieged by the Welsh, a prisoner in his own castle in Conwy over Christmas 1294.

The garrison – and the king – came close to starving to death. Although the uprising was defeated in 1295, it had proved that these castles built by the crown provided only a foothold in Wales. Other rebellions in future would underline that the country was not always under the control of those behind the walls.

Caer Drewyn and Ruthin

Location: Caer Drewyn and Ruthin town
Battle: Welsh (*Owain Glyndŵr*)/English
Date: 16–18 September 1400

Caer Drewyn is an Iron Age hill fort on the western spur of the hills between Llangollen and Corwen. It overlooks the confluence of the rivers Dee and Alwen, affording control of those valleys, and the Berwyn to the south.

According to Edward Llwyd, the Welsh used to keep cattle in it during times of war. Tradition has it that Owain Gwynedd assembled regiments from all parts of Wales there, when leading the 'One Wales army' in 1165.

There is also a strong tradition that this was where Owain Glyndŵr gathered his army of 300 together before attacking Ruthin (*Rhuthun*) on 18 September 1400, thereby starting a rebellion that would last for fifteen years.

Following Madog ap Llywelyn's 1294–95 revolt, tougher penalties were again inflicted on the Welsh. Heavy taxes were levied and a new castle was built at Beaumaris. After twelve centuries of attack on the country, it's little wonder that there are more castles per square mile in Wales than anywhere else in the world – over 500 castles have been recorded, and there are many more wood and earth defences that were never replaced by stone.

The invaders' intention was to rule the Welsh by violence and terror from the safety of the castles. The accounts for one of these castles (Hope Castle Account of 1282) show Edward I paying a 'gift of the king' of one shilling for each Welsh rebel's head brought back by garrison troops after a day's hunting Welshmen in the surrounding areas. These records, for summer and autumn 1282, are tight columns on a 33-foot roll of parchment. Among them are 27 such payments made to soldiers who had caught Welshmen.

Over the next century, hostility grew between the Welsh and the alien administrators, exploding into riot and the occasional local uprising. In the 1370s there was anticipation that Owain Lawgoch (Owain 'redhand') – one of the Welsh exiles under the patronage of the French king – would return with an army to free the Welsh. Then, in 1400, a new

1. *Caer Drewyn; 2. Part of its defences*

Castles and towns of oppression:
1. Rhuddlan; 2. Conwy; 3. Beaumaris

national leader emerged who would lead Wales into the longest uprising in any country against the British empire.

He was Owain Glyndŵr (*c.* 1359–*c.*1415). He was descended from Powys princes through his father, Gruffudd Fychan, and Deheubarth princes through his mother, Elen. He was one of the minor Welsh lords with lands in Glyndyfrdwy, and Cynllaith, near Llansilin and his famous Sycharth court. He studied law in London and experienced a military career in the armies of Richard II.

He was not on good terms with the main English lord in north-east Wales, Reginald de Grey of Ruthin castle. De Grey was an English oppressor trying to steal land and riches for himself at the expense of the Welsh on the fringes of his lordship.

In 1399, Richard II was deposed by Henry IV, who declared his own one-year old son, Henry (Hal), Prince of Wales in a ceremony in London the same year. De Grey saw his chance to gain favour with the new king by demonising Glyndŵr and raising suspicion that he was still loyal to Richard II. In summer 1400, de Grey appropriated Welsh common land in the upper Clwyd valley, reaching to the Bwrdd y Tri Arglwydd boundary stones (Grid Ref. 104 468), the border of Glyndŵr's territory.

This was the last straw. Word was sent

out to the surrounding areas and on 16 September an army of about 300 Welsh assembled in Caer Drewyn, where Glyndŵr was declared Prince of Wales before the dean of St Asaph. This was a direct challenge to the ceremony in London the previous year. From the outset, therefore, this was a national uprising against the English king's authority in Wales.

But it was de Grey and the town of Ruthin that would suffer first. On 18 September, the Welsh army travelled from Caer Drewyn to Ruthin. It was market day there. The town was destroyed and burned. The army moved on quickly and on subsequent days attacked English strongholds the in the north-east: Denbigh (*Dinbych*), Rhuddlan, Flint, Hawarden (*Penarlâg*), Holt, Oswestry and Welshpool (*Y Trallwng*).

The great uprising of the Welsh had begun.

1. *Bwrdd y Tri Arglwydd;*
2. *Owain Glyndŵr memorial in Corwen*

Hyddgen

Location: Hyddgen, Pumlumon. Grid Ref. 909 792
Battle: Welsh (Owain Glyndŵr)/English
Date: June 1401

In response to the September 1400 uprising, Henry IV was furious and wanted revenge. He gathered a large army at Shrewsbury, intent on attack and destruction in north Wales in the early autumn. There was no sign of Glyndŵr and his army. Not a word. Henry soon returned to England empty handed, punishing the Welsh by passing Penal Laws in the London parliament.

In the spring of 1401, the rebels were busy again. On 1 April Conwy castle was captured by Rhys and Gwilym ap Tudur, Glyndŵr's cousins and ancestors of Henry Tudor ('Harri Tudur'). Glyndŵr himself was active in the west, his army growing. He petitioned the Welsh nobleman Harri Dwn, of Kidwelly, for his help 'to liberate the people of Wales from the bondage of our English enemies'.

By the beginning of June there was an army tracking the rebels, drawn from the Ceredigion English and south Pembrokeshire Fleming towns. With 1,500 men, they found Glyndŵr's camp in the Hyddgen valley on Pumlumon. So far, lightning attacks and skirmishes had been the pattern of the rebellion. Hit and run and hide were the strengths of the Welsh against a strong network of castles and sizeable armies. At Hyddgen Glyndŵr had to fight his first set battle and it was key. Since September 1400, this leader had been an outlaw in his own country. If he lost the day at Hyddgen he would be an outlaw without a stronghold and with declining support. A fugitive went into this battle; a prince came out.

Pumlumon is a plateau of upland marshy valleys, noted for its rain and mists. There are no high peaks or rocky ridges and large parts are still inaccessible and make for difficult walking. It was ideal terrain for Owain and his army: using their local knowledge of the paths and the passes the rebels could attack several royal towns and then 'disappear'. It was not suitable country for the enemy's knights.

Some historians say that the appearance of the English/Flemish army

1. Hyddgen valley; 2. Battle monument at Nant y Moch reservoir; 3. One of the Cerrig Cyfamod Glyndŵr ('covenant stones')

that June in the lower Hyddgen valley was 'unexpected'. It's more likely that Glyndŵr's scouts had been tracking it since its departure from the safety of Aberystwyth castle, some 20 miles away. More than likely the Welsh were also prepared for battle and would have chosen carefully the location and timing of the two armies' meeting.

Local tradition says that Glyndŵr's main camp was to the north of Mynydd Hyddgen (*Hyddgen mountain*), at Siambr Trawsfynydd (*'chamber across the mountain'* – now under a forest of conifers). Hyddgen valley itself, however, is open, treeless, rocky and marshy – very similar to how it was six hundred years ago.

Southwards, at the confluence of the Hyddgen and Hengwm, the valley floor is narrow – only two or three yards wide. There, about a hundred yards to the west of the river, at the foot of Banc Llechwedd Mawr, there are two white stones about two feet tall, twenty yards apart, and orientated north–south. According to the local historian, Cledwyn Fychan, these are the Cerrig Cyfamod Owain Glyndŵr (*'Owain Glyndŵr's covenant stones'*) (Grid Ref. 897 785). Some historians locate the battle to the south of the valley; others favour the broader north, at the foot of Hyddgen mountain. As there is about a mile between them, fighting could have extended along the valley, as many of the English were killed in the rout.

Mynydd Hyddgen is a steep knoll with a flat summit, 1,850 feet above sea level, offering an excellent platform for a small army to keep watch. Several early descriptions of the battle locate it here and say that the alien army 'surrounded Glyndŵr's camp'. Glyndŵr would want to protect the site of his true camp, where the cattle and booty were, so he probably deliberately placed his army on Mynydd Hyddgen. He would, perhaps, have had about 120 mounted men – on mountain ponies and Welsh cobs: far more effective on rough terrain than the enemies' mounts.

It is possible that the battle took place late in the day, after the 1,500 had walked up the rugged valleys to the foot of Mynydd Hyddgen. It is possible that Glyndŵr manipulated this army, unfamiliar with the terrain, so that they were spread thinly round the edge of the mountain. Perhaps it was foggy, or maybe the sunset was dazzling the enemy by then. He would have chosen the best slope for his horsemen to race down and strike the enemy at full force. As it was such a sudden and blistering attack, the English had no time to form up their defence. A gap was smashed through the ring and soon the whole English army was fleeing, leaving over two hundred dead.

According to tradition every member of Glyndŵr's army pledged on the Cerrig Cyfamod to continue the fight until they had secured freedom for the Welsh. Certainly, the Hyddgen victory gave a huge boost to the rebels. It was recorded that Welsh students at Oxford and Cambridge abandoned their books and joined his army. Similarly, Welsh reapers returned from the harvest in England and took up weapons for the cause. His army went on to attack the mighty castles of Aberystwyth, Harlech and New Radnor (*Maesyfed*).

Henry IV assembled another royal army – this time at Worcester – to march to Wales in early autumn. They made the people's life hell by killing, burning and robbing, and they destroyed the great abbey of Strata Florida (*Ystrad Fflur*); but they had no military success. On the way back to England, the depth of their frustration and desire for revenge is illustrated by their capture of about 1,000 Ceredigion children, abducted in chains to live a life of slavery. The king retreated over the border to the pitiful sound of children weeping.

Bryn Glas

Location: Pilleth, New Radnor Grid Ref. 255 681
Battle: Welsh (Owain Glyndŵr)/English
Date: 22 June 1402

By the summer of 1402, much of Wales was in the possession of Glyndŵr and his followers. The English regiments were imprisoned in their own castles, impotent, unable to administer the country. The rebels had licence to assemble, travel and to strike the enemy at will.

One of Owain's armies was heading east towards the border in June 1402. In crisis, Edmund Mortimer, 26 years old and one of the strongest Marcher barons, mustered the Herefordshire troops. About 2,000 men and 500 knights gathered in Ludlow in the lower Lugg valley, including a regiment of crack longbowmen from among the Marcher Welsh. Up the wet and wooded valley this army marched.

The Welsh army waited for them on top of Bryn Glas, Pilleth and it's likely that Rhys Gethin of Nant Conwy, Owain's leading general, led that day. He had fewer numbers – perhaps around 1,500 – but his was a fleet, skilled army, suitable for the ground. Maybe some of its regiments hid over the brow of the hill, giving the impression that they were even fewer, to attract the English into the trap.

Mortimer's army began to climb the steep slope towards the church of St. Mary confidently. The land was not suitable for horsemen and that portion of the army was now ineffective. At a certain sign, they say, the bowmen amidst Mortimer's army turned their arrows on the enemies of the Welsh and Rhys Gethin's army pressed their charge downhill. The careful planning worked perfectly and it's believed 1,100 Englishmen were killed in the massacre, including some of their country's most famous knights. Mortimer was held prisoner. It was a resounding victory for the Welsh and it was said that thereafter the London English feared that Glyndŵr and his soldiers would occupy and wreak revenge on the whole of England.

Mortimer was offered to the crown for ransom, but Henry refused to pay. The

1. *Bryn Glas, Pilleth and the English mass grave marked by Wellingtonias; 2. St Mary's church; 3. The view from the top of Bryn Glas, as seen by Glyndŵr's army*

baron changed sides, joining Glyndŵr and sealing the alliance by marrying his daughter. Later, Glyndŵr, Mortimer and Percy – from northern England – created a tripartite agreement: they planned to divide the kingdom between them and threaten the sovereignty of the crown in London.

Thus began the best period for the Welsh uprising. Glyndŵr went on to win many battles and capture a number of castles. He set up himself up in the stronghold of Harlech castle and called an all-Wales parliament in Machynlleth in 1404, with representation from every commote. He made alliances with foreign kingdoms and outlined his vision for a Welsh government to administer the Laws of Hywel Dda, and with its church and educational institutions Welsh-speaking and independent.

Pwll Melyn

Location: Usk. Grid Ref. 255 681
Battle: Welsh (*Owain Glyndŵr*)/English
Date: May 1405

This was not the rebels' last battle and there were occasional victories for Owain Glyndŵr and his followers for over a decade afterwards. But the battle of Pwll Melyn in 1405 marks the tide starting to turn against the Welsh. The majority of the country is still free and Aberystwyth and Harlech castles would not fall into the hands of English – using cannons, fired for the first time in the history of warfare in Wales – until 1408–09. An economic blockade and starving the Welsh is what eventually took the wind out of the sails of the rebellion, not victories in battle. Owain refused to surrender or accept an offer of a pardon. He lived, outlawed, with a small group of the faithful before he completely disappeared from public view. He raised hope and confidence in the hearts of Welsh and that was enough to keep his dream alive for centuries after his life and his career.

Yet, there's no doubt that losing the battle of Pwll Melyn was devastating for him, undermining the confidence of his followers and grieving him personally.

A band of Owain's raiders, led by his brother Tudur and his eldest son, Gruffudd, was approaching Usk (*Brynbuga*) from the north-east along a ridge of hills. They were on a sortie in Monmouthshire, burning enemy castles and towns. There were not many of them, and they were probably lightly equipped for sudden attack and moving on quickly.

Unbeknown to them, Prince Hal (Henry IV's son) and an army of 3,500 had left Hereford to strengthen the Monmouth castle garrisons and by early May he had reached Usk, with Welsh arch-traitor – Dafydd Gam – as one of his guides. When they heard that the Welsh were approaching the town, a large English army went over the ridge above the castle to meet them. The Welsh quickly attacked them, but they were outnumbered. The battle turned in favour of the English and many of the Welsh were killed as they tried to flee.

Among the losses was Tudor, Owain's brother, and another experienced warrior called Hopcyn ap Tomos. Gruffudd, the

Area of the
Battle of Pwll Melyn
1405
✕
Maes Brwydr
Pwllmelyn

USK CIVIC SOCIETY 2005

Cymdeithas Ddinesig Brynbuga

Pwll Melyn ¼ m
✂
1405

eldest son, was captured in Monkswood forest and was taken to the Tower of London prison, where he died in 1411. Three hundred other Welshmen were caught and beheaded in front of the castle after the battle.

North-east of Usk Castle (right) there is a signposted path to the Pwll Melyn battle site and a commemorative plaque was placed there in 2005. At one time, in a hollow in the hills, this was a slimy and dirty pool and when it was cleaned to create a small reservoir for the railway below, many skeletons were found in it. Agricultural fields lie where marshy land has been drained, but on the valley floor the remains of the Monkswood forest, where many of the Welsh were pursued and caught after the battle, can be seen.

Llanidloes and Newport

Location: Llanidloes; Gwent Valleys
Battle: Chartists/Soldiers
Date: 1839

After Glyndŵr's uprising, there was not another armed uprising on Welsh soil between an army and the powers that be in London. Yet the issues he presented in that important document of 1406, the Pennal Letter – a letter to the king of France – were on the political agenda in Wales for the following six centuries.

For example, the Pennal Letter sets out Glyndŵr's vision for religious administration in Wales: that the church be independent of Canterbury and that the priests be Welsh-speaking. There were uprisings in other parts of the British Isles against the Protestant Church introduced by Henry VIII and Elizabeth I, but not in Wales. One of the reasons could be that the crown had commissioned an official translation of the Bible into Welsh. When it was published in 1588, it was the law that a copy be available in every church in Wales (and Welsh areas over the border), and that the priests were to use it every Sunday. Bishop William Morgan's classic translation was welcomed by the Welsh people and laid the foundation for modern prose in the language. When the Church in Wales disestablished in 1920, part of the Pennal Letter vision became reality.

In summoning several parliaments – in Machynlleth, Dolgellau and Harlech – Glyndŵr sowed the idea of a government with representation from all parts of Wales. When Wales voted for autonomy in 1997, and with the additional powers that the Welsh Assembly is consistently ensuring, decentralised democracy is now in place.

That journey has not been easy. Although women of the Gwladfa, the independent colony in Patagonia founded by the Welsh in 1865, had the right to vote (at least until the Argentinian state swallowed it twenty years later), women in Wales had to wait until 1928 for the London government to give them that right, and that after Wales saw a deal of activity in the women's suffrage movement. Another movement to extend

1. Market hall, Llanidloes; 2. The attack by soldiers on the Newport Chartists

suffrage was promoted by the Chartists. Between 1836 and 1842 their campaign was a reaction to changes in the population, mainly in the industrial areas. Although it was a movement throughout Britain and its six-point charter was drawn up by a workers' association in London, Wales saw the worst conflict.

Wales was the first industrialised country in the world and those industrial areas were uniquely Welsh in character. Chartists met regularly in the south Wales coalfield areas and also in the towns of the wool industry in the Severn valley; speech-making and petitioning was their approach. Nevertheless, the authorities assumed that protest would lead to violence and sent troops to those areas.

London police came to Llanidloes on 20 April, 1839 and a crowd of factory workers attacked their hotel. The Chartists controlled the town for a week, but then it was surrounded by cavalry and infantry soldiers were sent to search houses. Court cases followed, and three of the leaders were transported.

Five thousand Blaenau Gwent workers marched to Newport (*Casnewydd*) on 4 November, 1839. Living and working conditions in the industrial valleys were appalling and workers threatened to occupy and control the area by creating a regime of 'revolutionary activity which would sweep through the kingdom', in the words of John Davies. The marchers attacked the Westgate Hotel where there was a detachment of soldiers. The soldiers fired at the crowd from the windows and killed at least twenty Chartists. The leaders were brought before the courts and eight were condemned to death for treason. In the end, the sentences were commuted to imprisonment for five and transportation to Van Diemen's Land for the other three.

Merthyr Tudful

Location: *Merthyr Tydfil*
Battle: *Ironworkers/Soldiers*
Date: *June 1831*

Merthyr Tydfil (*Merthyr Tudful*) had grown to become one of the largest industrial centres in the world when the Crawshay family of Yorkshire set up the world's largest iron furnaces at the time in Cyfarthfa. Limestone, coal and iron ore were available in the area and there was enough turning power in the Taff's waters. A canal was opened to connect the Cyfarthfa furnaces and other furnaces in the area to Cardiff in 1794, significantly reducing the price of transport and creating a robust industry that would expand and create enormous wealth for the owners during the Napoleonic Wars.

By 1804, there were 1,500 employees in the Crawshay work at Cyfarthfa alone, and it was still expanding. Workers flocked there from all parts. Nights were red with furnace flames, and days black and yellow from sulphur gases and coal. Between 1800 and 1840 Merthyr's population grew from 7,705 to 35,000, and some parts were dirty and poor, with disease rampant. Cholera killed over 1,500 in 1849. On the other hand, the Crawshays spent a fortune on building a 'castle' for themselves in 1825, with 72 rooms for one family.

This is the essence of the early Industrial Revolution. Its undesirable side effects led to disturbances between the workers and the owners. There were mass protests and these sometimes led to violence. The most famous of these was the Merthyr Rising in 1831, when the town was occupied by the workers and the

Raising the 'Red Flag' in Merthyr

authorities sent soldiers of the 93rd (Highland) Regiment against them. Sixty of the protesters were killed and several soldiers were injured; one was killed. A young man named Richard Lewis – Dic Penderyn – was accused of killing the soldier and although the evidence was flimsy, Dic was hanged outside Cardiff (*Caerdydd*) prison on 13 August that year.

There were thousands watching the deed. In 1874, in America, another worker confessed on his deathbed that he had killed the soldier in Merthyr. Dic is remembered as the first martyr of the industrial workers and two sentences capture that turbulent period. Dic Penderyn's last words, having not eaten a bite of food after the sentence against him was passed, were 'O Arglwydd, dyma gamwedd' (*'Oh Lord, what injustice'*). The last words of Robert Thompson Crawshay who died in 1879 – the last of the ironmasters – were 'God forgive me', and that on his gravestone.

Unfortunately, Merthyr is not the only place where regiments of British troops have been used to attack workers in Wales. They have been used on several occasions when miners and other workers called for fairer wages and better conditions. In 1869, bringing in the troops forced miners from Mold (*Yr Wyddgrug*) to surrender to the power of the state and the bosses, and killed four civilians. There was a military intervention in the strike of 1900–03 at the Penrhyn quarry in Bethesda. Llanelli railwaymen were attacked – and two killed – in 1911 by more than 600 soldiers. When it was announced that Winston Churchill would be honoured by having his picture on plastic money in 2016, there was a storm of protest in Wales as Churchill was responsible for sending soldiers to put down workers in Tonypandy in 1911.

Heavy-handed state intervention continued in industrial disputes and there are bitter memories in Welsh mining communities about the miners' strike of 1984–85 when Margaret Thatcher armed the police in paramilitary style, using political power to break the strike.

1. Cyfarthfa Castle, Merthyr; 2. The grave of one of the Crawshays; 3. A memorial to Dic Penderyn

Efail-wen

Location: Efail-wen, west Carmarthenshire
Battle: The Rebecca Riots
Date: May 1839

At the same time as industrial disputes were happening in the coal and iron valleys, political and social drama raised its head in rural Wales. Carmarthen was a centre of radicalism, and poverty caused a riot there in 1831. Soon afterwards, rural west-Walians would express their dissatisfaction with their circumstances.

In 1839, a new tollgate was built on the turnpike road at Efail-wen, near the Pembrokeshire–Carmarthenshire border. A tollgate consisted of a gate across the road and a toll house adjacent, and the toll-collector collected money from everyone using the road. The aim of the system was to raise money to improve the condition of roads and build new roads, but the turnpike trusts were greedy. Gates were erected close together, resulting in considerable cost for each trip to market or to the harbour to collect coal and limestone. In 1833, a law was passed to increase the toll rates – and there were five turnpike roads leading into Carmarthen with rates of sixpence for a horse and cart, one shilling and sixpence for 20 cows, and a shilling for 20 sheep. During the same period market prices fell and rents were high. A mood of injustice swept through the countryside.

The first attack was at Efail-wen. Under the leadership of Twm Carnabwth (Thomas Rees) of Mynachlog-ddu, men in women's clothing, with blackened faces, gathered. The leader was called 'Rebecca', after the biblical character, the mother of 'thousands' who would possess the gates of those who hated them. This band, called the 'Daughters of Rebecca', marched with axes and implements of destruction to the new Efailwen gate in the early hours, destroying and burning the tollgate. Before the end of 1844 another 140 toll gates in west and central Wales would be destroyed and burned.

The rioting became more violent as it spread, and sometimes hundreds were involved. There were several different local 'Rebeccas' and historians believe that

Memorial to the Daughters of Rebecca's first attack, on the Efail-wen tollgate

GYFERBYN A'R GARREG
HON, AR Y 13EG O FAI
1839 Y DINISTRIWYD
TOLLBORTH AR Y FFORDD
DYRPEG AM Y TRO
CYNTAF, A THRWY
HYNNY DECHREUWYD
RHYDDHAU FFYRDD
Y WLAD

Hugh Williams, the radical Carmarthen lawyer, was the true leader of the riots, but only a very few of the activists were tried and deported.

More police and soldiers were sent to south Wales and rewards of between £50 and £500 were offered for information about the rioters, but Rebecca's network of spies shared information and outwitted the authorities. The cavalry would go off in one direction, and Rebecca would strike in another.

In June 1843, two thousand protesters gathered in Carmarthen and the insurrection was about to turn into open rebellion against the town's workhouse. The 4th Light Dragoons rushed to the town and attacked the crowd.

But the complaints were listened to in time. A commission was established and in 1844 it announced that farmers of rural Wales had a justified case. Illegal gates were taken down and a fairer system put in place.

The war of the Sais Bach

The Napoleonic Wars ended in 1815 and soldiers returned to a country where there was no work for them. Heavy industry was in recession because of the much-reduced demand for iron and steel for weapons. Moreover, the population increased – Ceredigion saw a growth of 20,000 in 30 years.

Thousands left the countryside for the expanding industrial areas, and others exercised their right to build *unnos* cottages on mountain common land. Under this old procedure, a family could establish a smallholding around a house built by themselves and their friends in one night. A large number of these houses were built at the beginning of the nineteenth century, particularly in Ceredigion, Caernarfonshire and Radnorshire.

Some landowners saw population growth as an opportunity to develop agriculture and make money by selling produce to the industrial areas. This brought the landowners and smallholders head to head, but the London law favoured of the landowners, of course. Laws were passed in parliament empowering noble families to enclose the commons and create large estates – which meant turning out poor families from their *unnos* holdings.

In 1812, there was a large population living in such smallholdings on Yr Eifl mountain near Llithfaen, Llŷn. In preparation for stealing the land by statue, officials were sent to survey it. The smallholders planned to prevent them. Using a large sea shell as a horn, Robert William Hughes, Cae'r Mynydd called upon the locals to come and prevent the officers from doing their job, once they arrived in Llithfaen. Hails of stones were hurled at the land surveyors. But before long the Dragoons arrived and arrested some of the rioters and imprisoned them for six months. Another riot occurred in March 1813 and this time the Dragoons caught Robert Hughes and another leader; they were sentenced to be hanged. That was later changed to transportation for life to Botany Bay. The common land was

Cae'r Mynydd, Llithfaen

appropriated by the landowner to create sheep fields, but the ruins of Cae'r Mynydd can still be seen.

This was the pattern throughout Wales. At the end of the Napoleonic Wars, 50,000 acres of land was enclosed this way in Breconshire and Cardiganshire (Ceredigion) alone. That was the cause of conflict in the Mynydd Bach area of central Ceredigion. In 1816, parliament ruled that 5,000 acres of mountain common land could be stolen. Many residents lost their *unnos* houses, and their cultivation and grazing rights. Officials were pelted with stones there too.

Then came a rich Englishman named Augustus Brackenbury who bought 850 acres of this land at Mynydd Bach. He was a short, stubborn man, and was given the name the 'Sais bach' ('*little Englishman*') by

the Welsh. In 1820 the Sais Bach and his employees began building a sizeable mansion on the former common, but every night the Welsh would come and demolish it. Brackenbury employed tough guards to protect his property and things went from bad to worse. On July 11, a large 'army' of locals, some in women's clothing, their faces concealed, came to attack the mansion. The Sais Bach was dragged from his house and it was burned to the ground. Brackenbury offered £100 for the names of the mob, but no one was betrayed.

But the Sais Bach was stubborn. He started other buildings on his land, including one with castellations and a moat. Six hundred men rushed down from the mountain on 24 May 1826, bridged the moat and destroyed the house. Two years later, Brackenbury gave up trying to exercise his 'rights' and returned to England.

Land and property remained contentious in Wales. Several times over the last two hundred years, people have had to battle in attempts to get the authorities to respect their rights to live and work on the land, and this is a bone of contention.

Such a conflict was the 'Tithe War'. Traditionally, in the Middle Ages, the Catholic Church claimed a tenth of what the land produced. However, after Henry VIII's Protestant Reformation, that tax passed to the Church of England or the landowner. By 1880, the vast majority of the Welsh had turned their backs on the Church of England and worshipped in their own, independent Welsh chapels. The tithe was resisted, especially when there was pressure on agriculture. In 1886, farmers in the Vale of Clwyd refused to pay the tithe and bailiffs were sent to their farms to distrain stock equivalent to the value of the tithe. A large crowd of farmers challenged the bailiffs and stopped the auctions. Unrest spread through the countryside of Wales; the most serious incidents occurred in the summer of 1887 at Llangwm, when hundreds of farmers and policemen clashed, and the auctioneer was threatened with drowning in the river. There was a court case, and a political campaign by the Welsh radical press and Welsh MPs, and in 1891 a law was passed obliging the landowner, not the farmer, to pay the tithe.

The Mynydd Bach area in central Ceredigion

Penyberth

Location: Penrhos, near Pwllheli, Llŷn
Battle: Welsh/London Government
Date: 8 September, 1936

During the twentieth century, during both war and peace, the London government has used its to 'right' to occupy land in Wales for use by the armed forces, turning locals out of their homes and off their farms. One of the saddest examples of this was Mynydd Epynt in Breconshire in 1940, when the War Office took possession of 40,000 acres of excellent pasture. Eighty families –400 people – were turned off their farms. The Ministry of Defence still holds it and it has been contaminated with explosives forever.

In 1946, over half a million acres of Wales was in the hands of the War Office – a tenth of the country's land. In 1951, London tried to add 10,000 acres to the thousands of acres the armed forces already had at Trawsfynydd, but peaceful protest was successful there. Under Plaid Cymru's leadership, the road to the camp was closed for two days. Between 1946 and 1948, there was a successful campaign in the Preseli mountains in Pembrokeshire to prevent 60,000 acres from falling into the clutches of the War Office. Through constitutional campaigning, the grip of the military was slackened on two-thirds of the lands it held in Wales.

But this wasn't the case at Penrhos near Pwllheli. On 1 June, 1935, the London government announced it was setting up a weapons camp, airfield and bombing school at Penyberth mansion in Llŷn. There had been a local and national campaign to oppose this, with local government, MPs, and national, literary and religious organisations strongly opposed. Two sites in England had been considered, but ruled out: Northumberland (because the area is home to a special duck) and Dorset (swans).

By August 1936, half a million Welsh people had expressed their opposition to the plan, stressing the historic importance of Llŷn and its Welsh-speaking social structures. But demolition of the mansion and land clearance for the military camp went ahead.

In the early hours of 8 September, 1936,

'Penyberth Three' memorial at Penrhos

flames rose into the night sky above the bombing school sheds. The sky was red as three of the leaders of Plaid Cymru at the time knocked on the door of Pwllheli police station to state that they were responsible for the fire which, by now, had totally destroyed the bombing school. With the help of a few unknown supporters, they had carried explosives and detonators to the camp and within a few minutes it was an inferno.

The court proceedings that followed gave the opportunity for the 'Tri y Tân yn Llŷn' (the *Llŷn fire three*), as they became known – Saunders Lewis, D. J. Williams and Lewis Valentine (lecturer, teacher and minister) – to argue their case and present their reasons. Caernarfon Assizes failed to

1936 – 1986
HANNER CANMLWYDDIANT
LLOSGI'R YSGOL FOMIO
GAN
D.J. WILLIAMS · LEWIS VALENTINE · SAUNDERS LEWIS
'Fel y cadwer i'r oesoedd a ddêl,
y glendid a fu'

agree a verdict and the authorities moved the case to the Old Bailey in London, where they were sentenced to nine month's imprisonment.

Fifteen thousand came to Caernarfon pavilion to welcome the three on their release from prison and Wales did not forget Tân yn Llŷn: direct action against property, yet without endangering lives. That direct action – exactly four hundred years since the Act of Union joining Wales to England – was an inspiration in the last half of the twentieth century to political campaigns for self-government and law-breaking Welsh language campaigning.

By the second half of the twentieth century, economic imperialism meant that wealthy families from England could afford to buy property as second homes in Welsh coastal and rural villages while the local Welsh were unable to afford their first family home. There were mass protests and the slogan was 'Tai a Gwaith i Gadw'r Iaith' (*'housing and work to keep the language'*), as the loss of families from Welsh areas undermines the Welsh social structure there. Holiday homes were occupied by members of Cymdeithas yr Iaith (*'Welsh language society'*), with locals bringing them food. But protective measures designed to assist the local communities receive housing in their own areas failed to materialise.

By the late 1970s the gap between wages and property values in rural Wales and the cities of England was at its widest. There were 7,700 holiday homes in north Wales alone, with half of those in Llŷn and Eifionydd. In several villages more than half the houses were holiday homes. The referendum of 1 March 1979 decided against devolving power to Wales, and by May Margaret Thatcher and her Tory extremists were in power. There was no way to protect Wales's land and communities.

Then, in the early hours of 13 December, there was a fire at Tyddyn Gwêr, a holiday home on Mynydd Nefyn, and another in Llanbedrog. Within a few days, another was burned in Pennal, near Machynlleth and two others in Llanrhian, Pembrokeshire. The house-burning campaign was underway. By the end of the first month, there were 22 fires the length and breadth of west and central Wales; within a year the number had increased to 50.

Remains of holiday homes following the Meibion Glyndŵr campaign

On 6 February 1981, a letter arrived at the BBC's Bangor office from an organisation called 'Meibion Glyndŵr' (*'sons of Glyndŵr'*) accepting responsibility for the attacks. The burnings continued until the early 1990s, damaging over 200 holiday homes. However, despite the presence of the secret services in Wales, a reward of £80,000 for information, and the arrests of many prominent nationalists, no one from Meibion Glyndŵr was held for burning holiday homes.

Although covert activity was the hallmark of the movement, there was clear public support for the Meibion – obvious in the songs, t-shirts, cartoons and poetry of the period. The economic, linguistic and social problems were not solved politically, but with recession affecting house prices by the end of the 1980s, house-burnings ceased.

Llangyndeyrn

Location: Cwm Gwendraeth Fach
Battle: Welsh/Swansea Co-operation and the law
Date: 1959–64

Between 1880 and 1965, several English cities commandeered valleys in Wales, creating reservoirs and obliging the local Welsh to leave their homes.

The old village of Llanwddyn, a number of farms and smallholdings and 1,120 acres of agricultural land were drowned to create the Vyrnwy (*Efyrnwy*) reservoir in Montgomeryshire in the 1880s to provide Liverpool with water. Between the 1890s and 1952, five giant dams were built in the Elan and Claerwen valleys near Rhayader (*Rhaeadr Gwy*) to dam water for the Birmingham area. A parliamentary act gave that city's corporation the right to force people to leave their homes to make way for the lakes, without the need for planning consent from any Welsh authority. A hundred people were moved from those valleys, with only the landowners receiving compensation.

A valley on the Denbigh Moors (*Mynydd Hiraethog*) was flooded in 1909–21 to create Llyn Alwen for Birkenhead's thirst, and the Clywedog reservoir near Llanidloes was begun by another act of parliament in 1963. Despite strong local opposition, 615 acres of agricultural land was submerged.

Perhaps the most famous is the Tryweryn valley. Liverpool forced 48 people to leave the village of Capel Celyn, near Bala, destroying a chapel and a school, and flooding 800 acres to create a reservoir. Parliamentary power was again used to enforce the plan. There were extensive protests and attacks on the construction. In 2005, Liverpool offered a formal apology for hurt caused to the people and land of Wales.

On a national scale, the strongest objection was in the Tryweryn valley. But here too, Wales as a whole felt she had no power to resist any kind of decisions made by the English, if they so chose to submerge their valleys. The Pwyllgor Amddiffyn Tryweryn ('*Tryweryn defence committee*') was formed with the support of several organisations and prominent individuals; the mayor of Cardiff called a

1. *Tryweryn valley dam;*
2. *Elan valley dam;* 3. *Clywedog dam*

protest meeting attended by 300 representatives from local authorities, trade unions and others to express their opposition. The Liverpool Corporation Act, 1957, which allowed the flooding, received royal assent on 1 August, 1957 and every MP from Wales, except one, had voted against it; it was carried by members from England. Work began on clearing the land and building the dam.

But protest continued in Wales. Tryweryn grew into a powerful symbol of the whole nation. However desperate the fate of the valley, by then the final sombre chapters were playing out in public: closing the school, the final chapel service, farm sales, the residents leaving. The political heat rose in Wales and campaigning for the rights for Welsh people and the Welsh language began on several fronts.

In February 1963, three activists planted a bomb under the Tryweryn construction site's transformer. Equipment was damaged, but heavy snow meant the three were tracked and imprisoned. Llyn Celyn reservoir was opened on 28 October, 1965 but the Lord Mayor of Liverpool and his guests were forced to retreat unceremoniously when a crowd of protesters disrupted activities.

Later in the 1960s, the wrong done to the valley was kept alive with 'Cofia Dryweryn' ('remember Tryweryn') slogans across Wales, and by terrorist attacks on pipes carrying Welsh water to England. Between 1966 and 1968, there were six explosions causing major damage, halting water to English cities for a while. In 1970, the secret services discovered that MAC (Mudiad Amddiffyn Cymru – 'movement for the defence of Wales') was responsible and John Jenkins, its leader, was imprisoned for ten years.

This was the backdrop to the threat to Cwm Gwendraeth Fach in the early 1960s. But the people of the valley had learned important lessons from the way the authorities treated the Tryweryn residents. Almost all of the farmers owned their own land and, as one, under the wise guidance of their local minister Rev. W. M. Rees and representatives of the agricultural unions, they refused to allow Swansea Corporation officials to inspect or even walk on the land.

1. Map of terrorist attacks 1966–68, including those on pipelines carrying water from Wales to England; 2. Llangyndeyrn memorial

Swansea went to court to get statutory rights to explore the land but – facing trial and imprisonment – the residents stood firm, blocking entrances with old farm machinery, and chaining up gates. In the summer of 1963, the police were brought to the valley to try to force the inhabitants to surrender to court orders, but again the local population did not give in. In the face of such strength, Swansea gave up its plans to drown the villages and fertile land of Cwm Gwendraeth Fach.

After that, representatives of the valley defence committee addressed and shared information with areas of mid-Wales that were facing similar threats. This battle over Wales's land had been won.

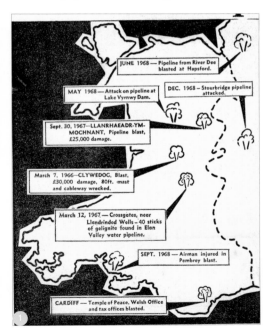

Battle for the Welsh Language

This is a very different fight from the other battles related in this volume. Geographically, it is the battle for the whole of Wales, but mainly the battle is in the very soul of Wales. In the end, the people of Wales will decide the fate of this battle through their commitment to use the language in all aspects of their lives or not.

On the journey to that point, a number of smaller fights dealing directly with the laws of the land had to be faced. This was a fight where weapons of violence were not used, but various members of the language movement became consistent lawbreakers over the years. From 1952 to 1960, the Beasley family of Llangennech fought to obtain a rate demand in Welsh from the local council. When their request was refused, the family refused to pay the rate. They were dragged to court 16 times and bailiffs visited the home four times to seize furniture to pay the rate. In the end the council gave in and provided bilingual demands.

After the establishment of Cymdeithas yr Iaith (*'Welsh language society'*) in 1962, this kind of civil disobedience became a common pattern in Wales. Between 1962 and 1992 there were 1,105 members of the organisation brought before the courts and 171 of them imprisoned. The emphasis was on breaking laws in order to draw attention to injustice and accept the consequences, leading to a growing consensus in favour of the Welsh language throughout Wales and the right to use it.

Laws were passed in 1967, 1993 and 2011 to strengthen the official status and equality of Welsh in law. Since the Act of Union in 1536 the law had banned the Welsh language from public life, administration of the law, and education.

It was legislated that no 'person or persons that use the Welsh speech or language shall have or enjoy any manner of office or fees within this Realm of England, Wales or other of the King's Dominion ... unless he or they use and

1. Plaque on the Beasley's home to commemorate their campaigning for the rights of Welsh speakers; 2. Protest against the Englishness of the Post Office

exercise the English speech or tongue'.

After centuries of exclusion, ridicule and being undermined, which led to a decline in Welsh people's confidence and willingness to use the language, Welsh is now reinvigorated. Nevertheless, creating the appropriate society and the state mechanisms where it can be used naturally and unimpeded remains a challenge. This is a battle that continues.

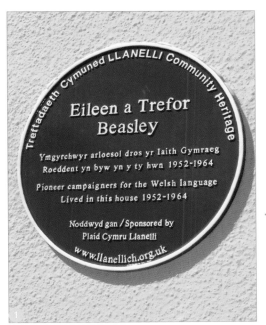

Sources

Historians are referred to by name in the text, and here are the sources of the facts cited:

Annales Cambriae, (History of the Welsh) a chronicle of genealogies of the Welsh probably recorded in St Davids by Owain ap Hywel Dda about 960

ap Rhys, Gweirydd *Hanes y Brytaniaid a'r Cymry*, Cyf. 1 a 2, William Mackenzie, 1872

Bede, Ecclesiastical History of the English People (*Historia Ecclesiastica Gentis Anglorum*), written around 731

Charles-Edwards, T. M., *Wales and the Britons 350–1064*, Oxford University Press, 2014

Davies, John, *A History of Wales*, Penguin, 1994

Fleming, Ian, *Glyndŵr's First Victory – The Battle of Hyddgen 1401*, Y Lolfa, 2001

Geoffrey of Monmouth, *Historia Regum Brittanniae* (History of the Kings of Britain), about 1136

Gilbert, A., Wilson, A. & Blackett, B., *The Holy Kingdom*, Bantam Press, 1998

Griffiths, Jenny and Mike, *The Mold Tragedy of 1869*, Gwasg Carreg Gwalch, 2001

Gruffydd, Alwyn, *Mae Rhywun yn Gwybod ...*, Gwasg Carreg Gwalch, 2004

Hackett, Martin, *Lost Battlefields of Wales*, Amberley, 2014

Jones, Arthur (ed.), *The History of Gruffudd ap Cynan*, Manchester University Press, 1910

Hughes, Vaughan, *Cymru Fawr: Pan oedd gwlad fach yn arwain y byd*, Gwasg Carreg Gwalch, 2014

Huws, Howard, *Buchedd Garmon Sant*, Gwasg Carreg Gwalch, 2008

Jones, Craig Owen, *The Revolt of Madog ap Llywelyn*, Gwasg Carreg Gwalch, 2008

Jones, David, *Before Rebecca – Popular Protests in Wales 1793–1835*, Allen Lane, 1973

Lloyd, J. E., *A History of Wales*, Vol. 1, Longmans, Green & Co., 1911

Mwyn, Rhys, *Cam i'r Gorffennol: safleoedd archaeolegol yng Ngogledd Cymru*, Gwasg Carreg Gwalch, 2014

Nennius, *Historia Brittonum* (History of the Britons), written in Gwynedd 796–830/about 830

Phillips, Dylan, *Trwy Ddulliau Chwyldro ...? Hanes Cymdeithas yr Iaith Gymraeg 1962–1992*, Gomer, 1998

Rees, W. M., *Sefyll yn y Bwlch*, Y Lolfa, 2013

Richards, Melville, *Enwau Tir a Gwlad*, Gwasg Gwynedd, 1998

Roberts, Gomer M., *Crogi Dic Penderyn*, Gomer, 1977

Smith, J. Beverley, *Llywelyn ap Gruffudd – Tywysog Cymru*, Gwasg Prifysgol Cymru, 1986

The Anglo-Saxon Chronicle, a portrayal of the establishment of the English

Turvey, Roger, *Owain Gwynedd, Prince of the Welsh*, Y Lolfa, 2013

Turvey, Roger, *Twenty-one Welsh Princes*, Gwasg Carreg Gwalch, 2010

Rees, Rice, *Welsh Saints or the primitive Christians*, 1836

Warner, Philip, *Famous Welsh Battles*, Fontana, 1977

Ten Birthdays

KERRY WILKINSON

bookouture

Published by Bookouture
An imprint of StoryFire Ltd.
Carmelite House
50 Victoria Embankment
London EC4Y 0DZ
www.bookouture.com

ISBN: 978-0-34913-242-6
eBook ISBN: 978-1-78681-172-1

Printed and bound in Great Britain by Clays Ltd, Elcograf S.p.A.

Papers used are from well-managed forests
and other responsible sources.

This book ... ses,
organizatio ... the
public doma ... ation
or are used fi ... ving or
de ...